The TREASURE OF MONTSEGUR

Walter Birks
read History at Oxford and after military service in the
Second World War had a distinguished teaching career
in the Middle East. He is the author of a standard history
of Islamic Egypt. Now retired, he lives at Bath, in Avon.

R. A. Gilbert
read Philosophy and Psychology at the University of
Bristol and is an antiquarian bookseller with a long-
standing interest in the Western Mystery Tradition. He is
the biographer of A. E. Waite, a bibliography of whose
writings he has also compiled, and the author of *The
Golden Dawn: Twilight of the Magicians* and *The Golden Dawn
Companion*.

Dear Bill,

This is the story
of the Cathars - the
group of people I
mentioned to you, when
you reputedly
performed chivalrously.

Love,
Carol

The fortress of Montségur

The TREASURE OF MONTSEGUR

A Study of the Cathar Heresy and the Nature of the Cathar Secret

WALTER BIRKS AND R.A.GILBERT

Crucible

First published 1987

British Library Cataloguing in Publication Data

Birks, Walter
The treasure of Montségur: a study of
the Cathar Heresy and the nature of the
Cathar Secret
1. Albigenses
I. Title   II. Gilbert, R. A.
273'.6   BX4891.2

ISBN 0-85030-424-5

*Crucible is an imprint of The Aquarian Press,
part of the Thorsons Publishing Group,
Wellingborough, Northamptonshire, NN8 2RQ, England*

Printed in Great Britain by
Woolnough Bookbinding Limited,
Irthlingborough, Northamptonshire

3   5   7   9   10   8   6   4   2

Contents

List of Illustrations

Introduction

THE traveller who passes along the road between Lavelanet and Foix in the foothills of the Pyrenees can only stop and gaze in wonder when he sees, for the first time, the fortress of Montségur, crouching beastlike on the summit of a huge and isolated rock, five hundred feet above the floor of the valley it commands. The castle is now a ruin, but it was not always so, for in the thirteenth century Montségur was the citadel of Catharism, the heretical religious movement that flourished during the high Middle Ages.

Although it spread across southern France and northern Italy, Catharism was especially prevalent in Languedoc, to the extent that the condemnation of heretics by the Council held in the town of Albi in 1176 led to their being generally known as Albigensians. The heresy had its roots in much older religious movements, but no precise date can be assigned to its first appearance in Languedoc; its end, however, was another matter. In 1244 Catharism and all that it stood for came to a violent and catastrophic end with the fall of Montségur, but before the final surrender something infinitely precious to the Cathars was saved—or so it was thought both then and now. What precisely that something was is the subject of this book.

The first part of the book is concerned with what the Treasure of Montségur, for let us call it that, was not. Its real nature is considered in the second part, where the origins and nature of Catharism are discussed, its doctrines set out, and the sorry tale of its destruction by Inquisition and Crusade told. But why was it destroyed? Not simply and solely because it was a heresy threatening the Church and arousing the anger and greed of the secular state, but because Catharism claimed to be the only true expression of Christianity itself. It was, however, a strange and heterodox creed, grafting selected parts of Christian doctrine upon an ancient dualism that rejected utterly the essential humanity of Christ. Thus the Cathars denied the doctrine of the Atonement, rejected large parts of both Old and New Testaments,

9

and condemned Pope, priests, and sacraments alike. Such a faith, that not only renounced the material world but denounced it as evil and generally cast out all that was dear to the hearts—and, some would say, to the pockets—of the orthodox clergy, could not hope to survive in an Age of Faith when the Church it opposed was the final arbiter of Truth. There was a dreadful inevitability about the end of the Cathars.

The Cathars, however, both wished and expected to survive. They wished it because *they* had the truth, and expected it because they were themselves Languedocian and had popular support from peasant and noble alike. The former admired the apostolic simplicity and rectitude of the Cathars, which contrasted starkly with the seemingly endemic moral turpitude of the orthodox clergy, while the nobility maintained a political distaste for the power of the Church and were content to support those who opposed it. A minority, perhaps a very small one, understood and approved the Cathar doctrines and actively embraced their faith.

But the weight of feudal society was against them, and much as the Church might disapprove of both the manner in which the Albigensian Crusades were conducted, and the more ruthless methods employed to crush the heretics, it both desired and welcomed the suppression of the heresy. So, by the end of the thirteenth century Catharism had effectively vanished from southern France and with it, save for the records of its enemies and a few fragments preserved by chance, all its own doctrinal works, its rituals, and its own curious versions of the Holy Scriptures. And yet there is something more, something that did not vanish.

In 1243 Montségur seemed, as it does today, to be impregnable and it was, indeed, safe enough from direct assault; but it was not invulnerable to the ingenuity of siege engineers or to the tactical errors of its defenders. Thus, on 2 March 1244, after ten months of siege, the Cathars of Montségur surrendered. For a reason that remains unknown they were permitted to remain in the castle, unhindered, for a further fifteen days before the surrender took effect. At the end of that time, those who refused to abjure their faith—more than two hundred men and women—were taken out and burned. On the evening before, four Cathars who had remained hidden in the castle left secretly and escaped down the almost sheer cliffs on which the castle sits, bearing with them the key to the Cathar Treasure. What it was that they took away can only be guessed at, but it was not the material wealth of the Cathars, for their treasures of gold and silver had been smuggled out in January to be hidden in the caves of the Sabarthès (the country around the valley of the Ariège). It is enough for the moment to remember that two hundred Cathars went willingly to their deaths, secure in the knowledge that all they held most

10

sacred— the true Treasure of Montségur—was safe.

For six hundred years no one sought for the treasure or even speculated on its nature, and when finally those who were curious did begin to seek they found only dreams. We shall consider what the treasure really was, but before that we must look at the dreams. And here Walter Birks is uniquely qualified, for he was deeply and directly involved in the dreaming itself, until circumstance altered his life and the reassertion of academic training changed his attitude to the dreams; but of this he must speak himself:

After reading History at Oxford and teaching in France and England, I sat for a time at the feet of Dion Fortune in the Fraternity of the Inner Light and was inspired by her to devote my life to the occult. In 1937 I was given explicit instructions from the White Eagle Lodge (affiliated to the Polaires of France and to the 'Great White Brotherhood' of Tibet) to go to the Pyrenees and recover the traces of the Brotherhood which had been exterminated there in the past. A great secret was there waiting to be revealed to the right brother and all my life until then had been a preparation for this task. My researches having led me to Ussat-les-Bains I was greeted by Antonin Gadal, the 'Patriarch of the Sabarthès', who told me that he had been awaiting my arrival in 'the year of the Grail'. Two years later, having designated me as his successor, M. Gadal enabled me to become Manager of the Spa and the Grand Hotel des Bains. This was intended to provide for my material needs while I pursued my spiritual objectives. Unfortunately, the fall of France and subsequent events rendered this material base unviable and, I fear, the experience of five years active service in war had an equally destabilizing effect on the 'dream'.

My own involvement with the Cathars and their would-be followers of today has been less direct. A continuing interest in the origins and historical manifestations of what is called the 'Western Mystery Tradition' had resulted in an especial interest in the Cathars. As a consequence of this I have attempted to acquire, over the years, such published works on them as appear to have either a scholarly content or a deliberately 'esoteric' approach. These works are not at all easy to find and I was both surprised and delighted when in 1982 Mr Birks offered me his own collection. In addition he offered me his own unpublished work on the Cathars, which proved to be a wholly original study. It seemed most appropriate that his historical and critical study should be prefaced by its personal setting, and the first part of this book is as much that setting as a critique of those seekers whose obsessions, preconceptions, and eccentricities have led—and are still leading—them astray in their quest for the Cathar Treasure.

By virtue of a combination of sympathy and scholarship Walter Birks found what others failed to find. It is of striking simplicity—and yet that very simplicity led to its remaining unknown for so long—but its nature requires that once it is known to one it should then be made known to all.

R. A. GILBERT

PART 1

1

From Cathars to Neo-Cathars

USSAT-LES-BAINS, in the valley of the Ariège, was once a thriving and fashionable spa. Over the last fifty years, however, the fall in the water table has greatly diminished its viability and it is now but a ghost of its former self.

The majority of Ussat's clientele has always been those who came for the treatment which the spa waters offer. But in the summer season there were frequently groups of visitors of a very different kind, who came from all over the world attracted by the Cathar story. Among them were occultists and esotericists of every variety, some—earnest, poor, and ascetic-looking—arrived on foot or on bicycles; others, wealthy and well-fed, arrived in imposing motor cars.

The spa had its own chapel beside the Grand Hotel du Parc et des Bains, and there, during the summer season, Mass was said for the benefit of the visitors by the curé of the neighbouring village of Ornolac. After Mass it was traditional for the spa manager to offer the curé lunch at the hotel. Sunday was also the day when the hotel put on its celebrated *Menu Gastronomique*.

Victor Mir, curé of Ornolac from 1913 to 1961, was a most saintly man, a true priest and a perfect exemplar of Chaucer's poor parson:

> Benign and wonderfully diligent,
> And patient when adversity was sent
> For so he proved in great adversity.
>
> Wide was his parish, with houses far asunder
> Yet he neglected not in rain or thunder,
> In sickness or in grief, to pay a call
> On the remotest, whether great or small,
> Upon his feet, and in his hand a stave.
> This noble example to his sheep he gave,
> First following the word before he taught it.

One could not but be struck by the contrast between this saintly man in his stained and faded cassock, which was almost green with age, and the glittering throng of well-heeled epicures who filled the dining-room. Was not the Abbé Mir the very epitome of the gentle, ascetic Cathar Perfect? Yet he was the Catholic priest while not a few of his fellow diners probably believed themselves to be, if not actually Cathars themselves, at least the spiritual descendants of Cathars.

But he knew what brought these neo-Cathars to Ussat rather than to anywhere else. Here were the Cavern of Lombrives and the caves of Ornolac, the opening up of which had blended reality with fantastic legend and woven the stuff that Cathar dreams are made of.

The eastern Pyrenees are limestone mountains and the steep sides of the river valleys that run through them are pockmarked with caves, the larger of which have been the home of both man and beast for some thousands of years. It is not uncommon to find within them either traces of prehistoric culture or the remains of more recent occupation. A number of the caves have been opened to the public and to supply a natural demand, guidebooks to them have been published for many years. Most of these are unadorned scientific and historical accounts of the caves, dull but reliable. Others, as we shall see, are otherwise.

While most of the early descriptions of the Pyrenean caves were the work of local scholars, one of the first English travellers to visit them recorded his impressions of the caves of Ussat, and of the cavern of Lombrives in particular, in 1859. That traveller was Charles Richard Weld, Tennyson's brother-in-law, who gave an account of a tour he had made during the previous year in his book *The Pyrenees West and East* (1859). Speaking of Ussat he says:

The geologist will find much to interest him in the Val d'Ussat. The gigantic limestone buttresses which rise on either side of the defile are honey-combed by vast caves, having the appearance of huge port-holes. These caverns assume all manner of fantastic shapes. The greater part are inaccessible to even the most enterprising mountaineer, a fact which the numerous birds screaming at their mouths seem to be well aware of; a few, however, may be visited by means of narrow paths and ledges fringed by box-trees, which are excellent hold-fasts to the climber of Pyrenean heights. Guided by a boy, and provided with a candle, I explored the largest of these caverns. It lies within the bowels of Mont Soudure, about two miles from Tarascon, and extends for nearly a mile within the mountain. The peasants of the Val d'Ussat, who are very primitive, and full of dark superstition, affirm that the recesses of the Mont Soudure grotto have never been explored, and that they penetrate the mountain for many miles. The cavern contains numerous stalactites, which are much finer than those found in the small grottoes near Ussat. I also saw traces of iron ore, but it does not exist in this cavern in sufficient quantities to repay the cost of working. (pp. 321–2)

In short, inaccessible and uneconomic; of interest only to the geologist then and to the tourist now. No word on the Cathars and no word on their treasure; but that link, between Cathars and caves, was about to be forged.

Histories of the Cathars, invariably called Albigensians, had appeared from the time of the Reformation onwards; at first with the intention of assailing either the Roman Church or the Reformers and invariably coloured by the writer according to his prejudices, but from the time that Dom Vaissette published his monumental *Histoire générale de Languedoc* in 1730, with genuine attempts at impartiality. By the end of the nineteenth century, when Auguste Molinier's revised edition of the *Histoire générale* appeared (in fifteen volumes between 1872 and 1892), the scholarship was meticulous and the objectivity unquestioned, but no Cathars were found in the Cavern of Lombrives; indeed, the only reference to treasure in the cave was a negative one, in that coiners had been surprised there in 1302, when the Crusade was still a recent memory.

But for the esoterically minded, as for the anti-clericals of the Third Republic, such histories were fatally flawed: their scholarship was too dispassionate and there were no rabid attacks on Rome. What they needed was *real* history that recognized the superiority of legend over recorded fact and realized the need to accept as true only that which supported the thesis and bias one wished to maintain. And in 1870 their need was met, for in that year Napoleon Peyrat, the Protestant pastor of Saint Germain-en-Laye, began to publish his *Histoire des Albigeois*: on the one hand an epic venture into Romantic history, and on the other a whip to flay tyranny in general and the Roman priesthood in particular.

Within two years the third volume had appeared, and in this Peyrat gave free rein to his imagination. For page after page he waxed lyrical about the ancient Cathar 'bishop' Amiel Aicard, who, in the year 1270, preached to the faithful in the cave cathedral of Ornolac; and about the horrors of the year 1328 when five hundred Cathars were pursued into the same underground refuge by the Seneschal of Toulouse and his army—they held the army at bay but gained their victory at the dismal price of being walled-up alive. Peyrat's style is priceless, as—in another sense—are his books, for they have become extremely rare, and although extracts are to be found in a few recent publications it is almost impossible to gain access to his original words. Their flavour, however, can be found in the work of one author whose imagination Peyrat caught and who, in turn, inspired later generations of would-be neo-Cathars both in England and in France. That author was Maurice Magre, in whose book *The Return of the Magi* (*Magiciens et Illuminés*, 1931) Peyrat's tale is concentrated into a brief chapter entitled 'The Cave of

Ornolhac'. Starting with officers of the Inquisition who 'were set over the hunting of the Catharists and had at their disposal packs of trained hounds', Magre pursues both his theme and the Cathars into the Cavern:

A great many of these wanderers travelled in the direction of the cave of Ornolhac, in which it was known that the Catharist treasure had been hidden. There was formed there a new centre, a new Montségur. But this one was as deeply hidden under the ground as the other had been conspicuous above it. The untiring Inquisition was unable to leave in peace the dark hiding-place of these wretched men. By agreement with the seigneur of Castelverdun, to whom the land belonged, troops were sent under the Seneschal of Toulouse.

Legend relates that as these troops were advancing, Esclarmonde d'Alion— either from pure heroism or in order to share the fate of a man whom she loved—galloped along the bank of the Ariège and, when she reached the steep path which led to the cave, left her horse, climbed the winding track on foot and joined those of her faith.

The cave had two entrances, both of which were surrounded, but the Albigenses climbed ladders (which they then withdrew) to a yet deeper and more inaccessible cave. It seemed to the Seneschal of Toulouse impossible to attack them there. He thought it wiser and perhaps also more humane to substitute for torture and the stake a silent death in the darkness. He had both entrances solidly walled up. For some time he camped on the banks of the Ariège. He waited. He listened for some sound to reach him from the granite interior. Then he left the mountain which had become a tomb.

The Albigenses must have lived for some time in the darkness, for they had turned the cave into a granary. Several bishops and many adepts were among them. In the silent darkness the bishops no doubt uttered the words which promised divine pardon as a result of the imminence of death and of the liberation of the spirit. No doubt they stretched forth their hands over bowed heads in the invisible gesture of the Consolamentum. And possibly as individuals and groups bade one another farewell in the darkness and Esclarmonde pressed close to her earthly lover, a miraculous light lit up the vault with its myriad hitherto lifeless crystals, the petrified oozings of the rock, the age-old stalactites. Possibly, by the miracle of love that joined them so closely, they attained all together, as it is taught in their religion, the abode where matter has no weight, water no fluidity, fire no heat, and where is enjoyed the blessedness of loving endlessly.

The mountain above the Ariège has kept the secret of the mass without candles, of the death without grave and winding-sheet. The book of Nicetas, which was kept among the treasure, the lovers' kiss, the bishops' gesture of blessing, must have petrified from absence of air. The last of the Albigenses, motionless, clothed in stone, still celebrate their final ritual amid dead vegetation and lustreless crystals in a basilica of darkness.

'Only this and nothing more.' Alas, there was more, for after two and a half centuries of peace, the walled-up Cathars were rediscovered in 1578 by their Protestant successors who, appalled at what they found yet recognizing the sanctity of the place, promptly resealed the vault. Two more centuries were to pass before it would be opened again, less piously, by bandits who, in 1802, conducted their own massacre of troops sent against them. Splendid stories all, but with not an atom of truth in any of them.

There were certainly Cathars remaining at the time Amiel Aicard is supposed to have preached in his cave 'cathedral', but there is no recorded trace of his being in Ussat—or anywhere else—in 1270. Similarly, there are no contemporary reports, or later ones, of the immuring of the Five Hundred in 1328; presumably Peyrat had access to Cathar archives that survived on some Inner Plane as unknown and inaccessible to latter-day historians as were the caves themselves to the people of the fourteenth century. As for the bandits and their massacre—a sensational enough event even for a time of war: they were alleged to have killed some four hundred soldiers—*they* have no mention in any known criminal or Departmental archives, and first appeared before the public in an article on Ussat and its baths published in 1842. It seems more than likely that the story was a mendacious attempt to encourage public interest in the history of Ussat and to bring custom to the baths. Certainly Charles Weld did not hear of it in 1858, even though such a bloodthirsty story would have been ideal for his chatty account of his travels.

Peyrat, however, may well have convinced himself that the bandit story was a garbled account of an earlier Cathar episode, as he convinced himself that human remains and other objects discovered at Lombrives in 1862 were those of his glorious martyrs. He chose to reject the opinion of the palaeontologist Felix Garrigou that the bones were undoubtedly pre-Roman, preferring to build upon a vague supposition of Garrigou's father, Adolphe—the Patriarch of the Sabarthès—that they may have belonged to people of the Dark Ages. Of Garrigou *père*, who was the foremost historian of the Ariège in his day, there is more to be said in a later chapter.

But although Peyrat was guilty of turning his wild imaginings into alleged 'facts', he had no desire to bring about a resurgence of Cathar beliefs. He was essentially a fervent partisan of the Languedoc, imbued with an extreme anti-papal streak as befitted his defensive Protestantism; and it was, according to his widow,[1] that same Protestantism that kept him out of sympathy with the faith of the Cathars 'whose heroism and patriotism filled him with enthusiasm'; their doctrines, she said, 'were separated from his personal beliefs by insurmountable barriers'. Could Peyrat have returned to Ussat in 1939 he would have been as puzzled by its pilgrims as was Victor Mir.

The presence of these pilgrims, the neo-Cathar faithful as it were, was indirectly due to the 'Occult Revival' of the late nineteenth century, which had come just too late for Peyrat and his work to be taken up by its enthusiasts: followers of Madame H. P. Blavatsky who joined the Theosophical Society that she founded in 1875. Besides, Peyrat's *Histoire des Albigeois* was never translated, and English and American occultists—unlike Madame Blavatsky herself—could comprehend no occult or spiritual truth unless it was presented to them in the English language. A further thirty years would pass before the Cathars, their ideas and ideals, began to enter the consciousness of English-speaking occultists. And when they did they came via Germany and the Christ-centred Theosophy of Rudolf Steiner.

Steiner was never happy with the Eastern obsessions of the Theosophical Society and preferred to see the spiritual development of mankind as linked to the spirituality of the West. For him, hidden wisdom descended from Atlantis to Egypt and thence to the secret traditions of Christianity, inevitably becoming centred on Christ, although Steiner's Christ was very different from the orthodox Son of God. Jesus of Nazareth, who died on the cross, was quite distinct from the mighty being who was the Cosmic Christ, and as the Cathars had apparently maintained a doctrine of more or less similar nature they must necessarily have possessed the truth. Nor was that all, for just as that truth had been lost with the fall of Montségur, so must it have been preserved in secret in order for it to be recovered today. Schools of Initiates—for such had groups of simple believers now become— had of necessity transmitted hidden truths in secret, thus keeping them safe from the persecuting zeal of the Roman and reformed Churches alike until the time came for their latter-day revelation through the teachings of Anthroposophy (as Steiner's variety of Theosophy was known).

Realization of the supreme importance of the Cathars was, however, slow in coming to the English-speaking world. Thus for the most significant period of its existence (from 1905 to 1930) the popular and—for occultists—influential journal *The Occult Review* published only one article[2] on the Cathars, but that made no claims for the survival of Cathar beliefs and evinced no response at all from its' readers. Not until they were linked with something else—with the Holy Grail—would the Cathars catch the popular imagination. Suggestions of such a connection had been made before,[3] only to be promptly dismissed as untenable by Grail scholars (e.g. A. E. Waite, *Hidden Church of the Holy Graal*, 1909, pp. 524–31). But in 1937 (*l'Année du Graal*) an association was founded that united both occult and orthodox scholars. *Les Amis de Montségur et du Saint-Graal*[4] had the anthroposophist Maurice Magre as president, an eminent historian, Professor René Nelli, as Vice-president, and the English occultist

18

Francis Rolt-Wheeler as secretary. Among its other founding members was Antonin Gadal, a schoolmaster from Ussat and a firm believer in the story of the walled-up Cathars. Although Montségur remained the central symbol of Catharism, these 'Friends' encouraged their supporters to recognize the importance of the Valley of the Ariége.

Gadal used his beliefs to good advantage, for he not only encouraged the neo-Cathars but also promoted the Cavern of Lombrives as a tourist attraction (he was, after all, the local *Président du Syndicat d'Initiative*, i.e. the Tourist Bureau). He also presented those beliefs forcefully in the first of his books on the Cathars: *Ussat-les-bains. La Cathedrale et les 3 Eglises des Cathares Albigeois* (1936). Fortunately for his peace of mind, Gadal died in 1962 shortly before the publication of Joseph Dengerma's damning indictment of the whole imaginary history of Ussat, *Les Cinq Cents Cathares emmurés de Lombrives* (1967). Not that Gadal would have been worried too much, for he had discovered even greater significance in the smaller caves that faced Lombrives across the Ariège, and it was in any event around this Hammer of the Sceptics that nearly all subsequent Cathar dreams came to revolve. We shall encounter M. Gadal more than once in this book.

2

White Eagle and the Polaires

SOME years before *Les Amis de Montségur* came into being, an awareness of the significance of Catharism was already growing in England—albeit slowly—among the members of The White Eagle Lodge, an esoteric Spiritualist circle centred on the mediums Grace and Ivan Cooke and their spirit guide, White Eagle. Their interest in the Cathars stemmed, indirectly, from a seance held at the W. T. Stead Library (a spiritualist foundation in central London) in January 1931.

At this seance Grace Cooke acted as the medium for communications from the spirit of Sir Arthur Conan Doyle, the discarnate Conan Doyle telling the circle that he had an important message for one of the sitters, a French occultist named Zam Bhotiva. At later seances Conan Doyle revealed that he was working (on the astral plane) with the Rosicrucian initiate who was the spiritual power behind Zam Bhotiva's group, *Les Polaires*, and that M. Bhotiva should seek help in the furtherance of his occult work from a centre in England that was under the direction of the Great White Brotherhood. This centre proved to be the circle around the Cookes that was to become The White Eagle Lodge.

The *Fraternité Polaire* (so named from the Pole Star which was used as their emblem) had been formed by Zam Bhotiva in 1929, but derived ultimately from a remarkable Italian occultist, Pére Julien, who—according to M. Bhotiva—had been, in 1918, 'translated' to the Himalayan monastery of the Great White Brotherhood. From this Himalayan retreat the high Adepts directed M. Bhotiva to found *Les Polaires*, rather as Madame Blavatsky had been directed by her Mahatmas, although the spiritual Master of the Polaires was not oriental but a powerful Rosicrucian adept whose aim was to utilize the Polaires in a great struggle against the forces of evil. Gradually—and doubtless helped by Conan Doyle's messages—Bhotiva and his Polaires moved away from 'Asia Mysteriosa' (as he called it) and concerned themselves increasingly with the esoteric traditions of the

West, particularly with such initiates as Cagliostro and the Comte de Saint-Germain, and most of all with Christian Rosencreutz, the founder of the whole Rosicrucian movement.

According to the Rosicrucian manifestos of the early seventeenth century, Christian Rosencreutz had, some three hundred years before, travelled extensively in the Middle East to gain esoteric knowledge, returning to his native Germany via North Africa and Spain. The Polaires were convinced that he had passed through the Pyrenees on his return journey and had stopped at the castle of Lordat in the valley of the Ariège. Here they came in 1931 to excavate the ruins of the castle and to try to recover the lost Gospel of John which they believed they would find, but despite enthusiastic encouragement from the castle's owner, the Countess Pujol-Murat, nothing was found.

In the following year they were joined by Ivan Cooke, enthused by Conan Doyle's appeal for 'Friendship between France and England', and excavation resumed, helped by the psychic perceptions of the medium. It proved no more successful than before and came to a dramatic halt when one of the Polaires was suddenly and violently attacked by demons. The Polaires may have been eager to possess the Gospel of John but they had no desire for demon possession and the party fled. This was evidently a battle in which the evil forces against whom the Polaires strove had won decisively.

Despite this setback, White Eagle (through his medium) recognized that something of great importance awaited discovery in the Ariège, and five years later, when the White Eagle Lodge was well established, he instructed two of his followers, Brother Nobleheart and Sister Minnie, to travel to southern France, accompanied by their son: 'The purpose is for you to make contact, with Walter, certain places in France which hold the Light Ray. You have to learn to discriminate, to look beneath the material substance and read or absorb the beauty of the atmosphere. There are places, and in the French Pyrenees there is the ancient home of a brotherhood . . . the Albigenses.' (Quoted from a *verbatim* record of a sitting with White Eagle on July 5th, 1937. The son, of course, is Walter Birks.) Perhaps feeling that they would be less liable to demonic interference, White Eagle now directed his followers to the Cathars rather than to the Rosicrucian Brotherhood, and gave detailed instructions for Walter's travels: 'Go right across France . . . Go to the South to near Ax-les-Thermes. Tell him to find the brotherhood which is now wiped out—the Albigenses. It is not easy, but he *will* find it. The point of your going is for him to contact the Inner Planes. You will be somewhere near the southern part of France. The home of the Albigenses is in the Pyrenees—the Mediterannean side. Run up that side of the coast near Carcassonne.' (Sitting of 5 July.)

Walter was impressed, and after the sitting he sought for information on the Cathars, discovering that little had been written in English and that much of what was available seemed to be somewhat speculative. Ax-les-Thermes, of which he had not heard before and which he assumed was an error for *Aix*, proved to be a real town, approached from Carcassonne, and 'what is more it was there that the leaders lived who after the outward suppression of the sect kept it alive as a secret society. There aren't many men living who know that!' White Eagle was clearly little less than omniscient: 'I think it is marvellous the way he spelt it and insisted it was Ax and not Aix as anyone would expect.' (W. B. to his parents, 9 July 1937.)

He would, perhaps, have been somewhat less impressed if White Eagle had chosen to tell him of Ivan Cooke's visit to Lordat—which is a mere six miles from Ax-les-Thermes—in 1932. This was, no doubt, an oversight on White Eagle's part, for one would not wish to impute to him the desire to appear omniscient with his intimate knowledge of this little-known corner of France. Unaware of this lapse, his three followers went off to the Ariège, visiting Ussat and its caves—and meeting M. Gadal—and returning to England in September for further instructions from White Eagle.

Walter now learned of the importance of Ussat, and was told to 'Penetrate to the caves, for in the cave you will find the secret of a brotherhood—of *the* Brotherhood', although he would 'have to work in the dark with only the light of your own spirit'. White Eagle also advised caution: 'The great point for you to remember is to work keeping your own counsel, *keeping your own counsel*', and warned against treasure-seeking: 'You will hear of buried secret treasure. Treasure lies in wisdom and love, remember. Never be persuaded to work purely for material treasure.' (Record of sitting, 29 September 1937.) White Eagle was presumably determined that Ivan Cooke's experience with the demons should not be repeated.

He was also insistent that Walter should keep whatever he discovered to himself: 'There is only one man for you to trust, and this is *yourself* . . . keep inviolate the secrets of your own breast.' This advice seemed somewhat strange, for White Eagle knew that Walter had already met Gadal, who was clearly important, and wished to work with him: 'You were led to meet a certain brother and you felt you had an affinity—a link? He was ready to receive you. He wants to pass the torch to you for further work and research.' The constant urging of White Eagle towards complete selfishness perplexed Walter, and he said as much, commenting that he felt 'it would hardly be fair to Gadal and Rinderknecht [a Swiss enthusiast who was also at Ussat] to take advantage of all their work and information and withhold from them what I get myself. You see, White Eagle, the caves belong to M. Gadal.'

At this White Eagle felt it best not to press the point: 'If that is how you see it we had better leave it. You have not understood our words.' Returning to the question of trust at a later seance (9 February 1938) White Eagle seemed to face both ways: 'Monsieur Gadal is a good and beautiful brother, but do remember there are two aspects in every human soul. There is the human, personal self and the higher, spiritual self, and occasionally one may react on the lower aspect. For this reason it is best to be very wise and quiet, not too open and free. It is quite different from being deceitful. But I do say that Brother Gadal is a great, beautiful, trustworthy soul. At the moment he is the Guardian, but he will pass away and you will be the Guardian. Yes, you can trust him.'

One cannot help suspecting that this somewhat devious suggestion was intended to disguise White Eagle's almost total ignorance of the Cathars. Spirit Guides and hidden Masters alike have a tendency to become discomfited when faced with either the cold facts of historical research or the practical problems of living in the real world. They fare much better when dealing with great spiritual truths.

Some months previous to this seance, Walter had been approached— at Gadal's suggestion—by Francis Rolt-Wheeler, the secretary of *Les Amis de Montségur*. Dr Rolt-Wheeler was an English writer on occultism who had settled, apparently for the sake of his health, in the south of France; he was also by far the most flamboyant of the many seekers after the Cathar secret. He edited the journal *L'Astrosophie* which he claimed to have 'built up to be the most important and largest (also in circulation) occult review on the Continent', and was nothing if not self-confident: 'I'm a very old hand at directing reviews, magazines and dailies mainly in America, and have many years' work on the occult line behind me.' He had written to invite Walter to join *Les Amis* and to become a member of its 'Editorial Council', which he felt needed English members: 'I do *not* consider Provençal scholarship sound on Holy Grail matters, due to their insensate idea that Wolfram von Eschenbach was the Holy Trinity and Jaques Molay rolled into one. In my judgment, this movement needs English and Celtic [Rolt-Wheeler came originally from County Cork] stock behind it. It will have it, because I'm accustomed to have the co-operation of big men.' (Rolt-Wheeler to W.B., 29 September 1937).

Walter replied, asking him what it was that Rolt-Wheeler wished him to do. The task was far from modest: 'My dear sir, you have a continent to plough. Otherwise put it seems highly likely to me that we have before us a piece of spiritual work comparable to the Protestant Reformation, or the Crusades, and leaders will be needed.' More immediately he needed help in translating material from *L'Astrosophie* into English ('Amis de Montségur stuff', as he called it), for although he had a 'gripping, vital nervous English style' and had 'written tons of books and cargo-loads of articles', 'I can't do everything.' (Rolt-Wheeler to W.B., 23 October 1937.) He also placed a rather different emphasis on the work than did White Eagle: 'Your first duty, as I see it, is to Gadal and Sabarthès. I don't know what you are doing in Ussat, what help you are giving M. Gadal, or how the land lies. But loyalty *always* stands first.'

By the time he received Rolt-Wheeler's request, Walter was back in Ussat helping Gadal to develop the caves and to further his studies of Catharism. He told Rolt-Wheeler that the English public was unlikely to show much interest in *Les Amis de Montségur*, save for a few individuals such as Colonel Charles Seymour—a prominent member of the Fraternity of the Inner Light—who had already contributed a series of articles on the caves of the Sabarthès to *L'Astrosophie*; in any case, he asked, 'how many people in England have ever even heard of Catharism or have more than the vaguest notions of the history and geography of Languedoc, much less Montségur and the Sabarthès?' This may have been unduly pessimistic, but not to such an extent as to justify Rolt-Wheeler's response: 'You're wrong as to England. It will go like a whirlwind—will be too big, if anything. Obviously, we won't thrust Montségur and Sabarthès down the English throat. But I am letting that develop. When the time comes, I'll give you the whistle and we'll both go "over the top".' (Rolt-Wheeler to W.B., 5 November 1937.)

The time, however, never did come, and White Eagle seems to have summed up Rolt-Wheeler with a fair degree of accuracy. At a sitting in February 1938 he replied to a question about Rolt-Wheeler by saying 'I may be wrong about these others, but it seems to me there is a lot of hot air.' Nonetheless, Rolt-Wheeler was still making grandiose plans, and adding lost gospels to the Holy Grail as a part of the Cathar treasure. He also arranged to meet Walter on his return to France in May, but the meeting was a great disappointment to both of them. Walter described the occasion in a letter to his family (1 July 1938): 'I have met the great Rolt-Wheeler, and anybody less like a great occultist would be hard to imagine. He is an even bigger scream in person than he appears to be from his letters . . . a bald-headed and corpulent old buffer . . . He began to sketch out how he had begun to re-organise the earth and how he proposed to continue . . . Although he is the world's greatest worker and has written an average of 3,000 words a day for the last 40 years, he has also found time to learn Hebrew and study the Kabbalah therein, and to read the *Book of the Dead* in the original hieroglyphics. He can cast a complete horoscope in three hours and produce his *Astrosophie* regularly in three days.'

Rolt-Wheeler was also quite sure that the caves at Ussat were of no significance and that the young man he had believed to be a worthy disciple was 'simply a lazy good-for-nothing who was frittering away his time dabbling with things he didn't understand.' But despite his vanity and inordinate self-esteem, Rolt-Wheeler was possessed of a good deal of cunning and he determined that *Les Amis de Montségur* should be his and his alone now that no suitable henchmen seemed to be in the offing to aid him against the local members and their unsound scholarship.

The General Assembly of *Les Amis* was held at Montségur on 12 July 1938 and proved to be both the first and the last. Rolt-Wheeler had obtained the proxy votes of over a hundred members who were unable to attend, and fully intended to use these to ensure his complete control over the association. He proposed a council of administration, consisting of himself, his companion Mme Belaz, and two other people unknown to any of the members present, this council to remain in office for five years, with full powers to run the association as it wished. With his proxy votes Rolt-Wheeler could ignore the protests of members who wished to know just *who* would be running their affairs and the proposal was adopted. To make matters worse, he was also able, by using the proxy votes, to approve accounts, even though they showed that of some 12,000 francs received by way of subscriptions, only 400 francs were to hand. There was no satisfactory explanation of what had happened to the balance.

All this was too much for the members who protested strongly, causing Rolt-Wheeler to fly into a rage, to forbid the hostile members to speak and, finally, to depart in a huff. The astonished speakers were left with no meeting to address, the thirty members present all resigned on the spot and *Les Amis de Montségur* effectively ceased to exist. Louis Palauqui, a distinguished local historian and Rolt-Wheeler's principal critic at the General Assembly, attempted soon after to found a new and less personality centred organization, but Gadal declined to help as he wished to have nothing more to do with Rolt-Wheeler—least of all as an object of recrimination by his erstwhile colleague.

If nothing else, the fate of *Les Amis de Montségur* had shown that organized spiritual quests were all too vulnerable to the baser aspects of human nature. The secret of the Cathars could only be learned by individual effort and by mutual co-operation in an informal way. *Les Amis* had not held corporate views about the Cathars, but there seems to have been a general tendency among its members to see Catharism as being closely related to the Holy Grail and for the treasure, perhaps, to have been the Grail vessel. For the seekers at Ussat, however, Catharism meant more than Montségur and its treasure: the caves of Ornolac would prove even more spiritually rewarding when their purpose was fully appreciated.

With the demise of *Les Amis*, Antonin Gadal turned his full attention to the caves. He was not only lessee of the Cavern of Lombrives but effectively the proprietor of all the caves, sixty in number, in the four surrounding communes. Of these caves the most important were those at Ornolac, and Gadal perceived a connection between them that had escaped the notice of all previous historians and Cathar sympathizers. His interpretation of their purpose was both original and extraordinary.

3

Gadal

THE year 1937 was, for *Les Amis de Montségur*, '*L'Année du Graal*', and 12 July was '*le jour fixé*'. As to what was tó happen on that day they were far from clear, but when Walter Birks arrived at Ussat later in the same month, Antonin Gadal, the proprietor of the Cavern of Lombrives which he had come to see, greeted him as 'one for whom he had been waiting'. In turn Walter saw Gadal as the Master whom White Eagle had told him to seek. It did not occur to either of them that the meeting might have nothing to do with destiny, but as it turned out, if the meeting was no more than chance it was to prove a most happy coincidence.

Antonin Gadal was a native of the Sabarthès, born at Tarascon in 1877 in a house adjoining that of 'The Patriarch of the Sabarthès', the historian Adolphe Garrigou (1802–97). As a boy Gadal sat—both figuratively and literally—at Garrigou's feet, reading to the old man, whose eyesight had become weak, and acting as his amanuensis. In this way he absorbed not only Garrigou's enthusiasm for the history and prehistory of the region, but also his abiding belief in the romances of Napoléon Peyrat—whom Garrigou knew well—and in the spiritual heritage of the Cathars. For Garrigou this heritage contrasted strongly with what he perceived as the cold formalism of the Roman Catholic Church,[1] and it was, too, a living tradition. Was not the hermit who had lived in a cave above Ussat during the early years of the nineteenth century a spiritual descendant of the Cathars?

This hermit was alleged to have been the same person as the unknown man who 'the second after the head of Louis XVI had fallen under the guillotine . . . rushed forward on to the scaffold, scooped up some of the royal blood in his hands, made the gesture of scattering it over the crowd and cried: "People of France, I baptize you in the name of Jacques de Molay and in the name of Freedom"' (Magre, *The Return of the Magi*, pp. 165–6.) The story of this act of posthumous vengeance would presumably have been brought back to the Sabarthès by Garrigou's grandfather, who had been in Paris as Deputy for Tarascon at the States General. His identification with the Hermit of Ussat seems to have come later—probably after the story was printed in Eliphas Levi's *Histoire de la Magie* (1860). In Lévi's version there is no necessary connection with the Templars, for the baptism with the king's blood was done 'in the name of Jacques and of liberty',[2] but he did suggest a connection with the Cathars. His 'unknown', however, hardly conformed to the Cathar ideal: 'A hideous and gigantic being, covered with a long beard, was to be seen wheresoever there were priests to murder. "Behold", he cried with a savage sneer, "this is for the Albigenses and the Vaudois; this is for the Templars, this for St Bartholomew and this for the exiles of the Cevennes." As one who was beside himself, he smote unceasingly, now with the sabre and now with axe or club. Arms broke and were replaced in his hands; from head to foot he was clothed in blood, swearing with frightful blasphemies that in blood only would he wash' (Lévi, *Histoire*, English trans., p. 424).

Certainly there was no 'cold formalism' about the practices of such a being, but one presumes that he changed his violent and unsavoury ways before retiring to lead the life of a hermit at Ussat. It is difficult otherwise to imagine the gentle Garrigou wishing to follow him in the role of Patriarch of the Sabarthès.

That title, in any case, was unofficially bestowed on Garrigou by his contemporaries in recognition rather of his work as a historian than as a neo-Cathar. But as he had succeeded the hermit in the role of Cathar Patriarch, so he wished for a successor to himself. He was disappointed in his own son, Felix Garrigou, who had no interest at all in Catharism (he had argued cogently and publicly that the human remains found in the Cavern of Lombrives dated from the Bronze Age, and that Peyrat's story of the walled-up Cathars was pure romance), and looked instead to Antonin Gadal to follow him as 'patriarch'.

At the time of Garrigou's death, in 1897, the young Gadal was entering upon his career as a schoolmaster and had little time to follow the alternative career of patriarch, but a serious wound received on active service during the First World War led to him curtailing his teaching activities. He then took up the post of *Président du Syndicat d'Initiative d'Ussat les Bains*, becoming at the same time lessee of the Cavern of Lombrives and of all the lesser caves in the district.

Peyrat's tale of the walled-up Cathars, widely disseminated by the literary efforts of Maurice Magre, undoubtedly encouraged pilgrims to Montségur to add Ussat to their itinerary; but the Cavern of Lombrives was already a tourist attraction because of its natural splendour, and it needed little development save the addition of such material benefits as handrails and electric light to ensure that it continued to be a commercial success.

This was not the case with the many small and relatively inaccessible caves that honeycomb the cliffs opposite Lombrives above the right bank of the Ariège. These caves do not form a single, connected system and do not possess the enormous vaults, spectacular chasms, and delicate stalactites of Lombrives. For Gadal, however, and probably for Garrigou before him, they had a spiritual significance far beyond any possible commercial value: they provided an essential and continuing link with the Cathars. Had not the hermit lived in a cave at Ramploque in the very centre of the whole series? And was he not one of a continuing chain of Cathar Patriarchs down to Gadal himself?

So Gadal believed, although there was not a shred of documentary evidence to support his belief. It is possible that there had been prehistoric occupation of the caves; some of them may have been used as refuges by the Huguenots during the Wars of Religion, and rock inscriptions within them probably date from this time (Huguenot fortification of the nearby cave at Bouan on the left bank of the river can still be seen); and the Cathar gold smuggled out of Montségur in 1244 was allegedly hidden in the caves of the Sabarthès. But that the caves of Ussat and Ornolac were important to the Cathars there was no evidence at all, and if the Cathars had ever occupied the caves no trace of that occupation remained.

None of this daunted Gadal, who remained utterly convinced of the Cathar connection and developed his own theory that the caves had played a central role in Cathar religious practices. According to this theory the Cathar *croyant*, or believer, did not attain the status of *Parfait*, or Perfect, simply by undergoing the rite of the Consolamentum at an appropriate time of his life, but only after passing through a series of initiatory rituals involving a symbolic passage from the material to the spiritual and a physical passage through the cave system of Ussat-Ornolac. Nor did this take place as a single ritual: the initiate advanced from one stage (and cave) to the next only after an appropriate growth in his spiritual understanding; indeed, many years might elapse before the initiate passed through the final stage of his spiritual journey and attained his goal of becoming a *Parfait*.

The caves were thus nothing less than a proving ground for would-be Cathar Perfecti. If Montségur was the spiritual beacon of Catharism, the 'Grottes d'Initiation' of Ussat-Ornolac provided its haven of refuge: 'un port sûr et tranquille'.

The initiate began his spiritual quest in the West, crossing the symbolic wall that divided matter and spirit and kept the profane away from the Cathar Mysteries, and entering the cave-church of Ussat. He then progressed, by way of interior passages and mountain paths, through the surrounding caves: the Chapel, the crypts, and the Acacia Cave where he saw the supreme Cathar symbol of the 'Way of the Holy Grail' carved in the rock.

In due course he proceeded eastwards to Ramploque, to the caves called Le Grand-Père and l'Ermite (the supposed home of Garrigou's patriarchal predecessor), completing the second part of his initiation in the three sacred caves of Keplèr, Mès-Naut, and Ka. For his third and final stage of initiation the future Perfect was conducted to the most important cave of all: the Bethlehem cave at Ornolac. His approach was by way of a symbolic door, beyond which was a large retreat house—long since vanished and leaving no trace at all save in the mind of M. Gadal, perhaps the most fertile soil of all for the cultivation of Cathar remains—and the entrance to the Chapel of Bethlehem itself.

Without doubt the most fascinating of all the caves, Bethlehem was the most holy Cathar Chapel in which the 'new Christ' was born and the initiate finally became a Perfect. Roughly rectangular in shape, some 26 feet by 13 feet, the principal entrance is at the western end, facing a natural pentagon set in the east wall of the cave. To the left of the entrance was a niche in which was kept the Holy Grail, while below the pentagon was a large granite altar on which was laid the Cathar Gospel of John. The supreme moment of this final ceremony came when the initiate stretched himself out upon the pentagon—to become 'the living reality of the Fivefold New Man'. He was now a true Perfect, no longer the Green Osiris, or mere dedicated seeker after enlightenment, but the Black Osiris, reintegrated at last with the Father.

All this was a revelation to Walter Birks, for the researches of M. Gadal were quite unknown to him and his knowledge of the Cathars had hitherto been derived solely from the published works of recognized historians, who had never recorded the proper names of the caves of initiation, who knew nothing of the apparent connection of the Cathars with the Egyptian Mysteries, and who never once mentioned Ussat by name. They neither did, nor could, speak of the Chapel of Bethlehem as did Antonin Gadal: 'Ah! if only it could speak and tell us what it has heard! If we could learn the "vast subjects" discussed in the shelter of that rock: "God, the Universe, Creation, the Fall, Christ's Salvation, Eternal Torment, the Conversion of Satan, the Extinction of Hell, the Astral Purgatory, the Migration of souls from Star to Star . . . !" If we knew the meditations of which the platform was so often and for so long a witness!'[3]

Gadal was indeed an inspiring speaker, and the power of his oratory, coupled with his utter sincerity convinced Walter that he possessed spiritual truths hidden from the multitude. Further, Gadal was only too willing to share these truths, and Walter settled in happily at Ussat to assist him with his work and to act, as befitted a potential patriarch, as his amanuensis.

This, however, was far from being his only task. He returned to Ussat in May 1938 and stayed throughout the summer and autumn, helping Gadal both with tourists at Lombrives and with the excavation of the smaller caves. Gadal had already discovered a plaque in the shape of a dove on the site of the Cathar retreat house and now proposed excavating the Bethlehem cave. Walter's task was to arrange for the rebuilding of a relatively modern wall across the approach to Bethlehem, providing it with a secure gate so that the cave would be protected from the merely curious.

Before work began on the wall, Walter was shown what had already been accomplished:

Today Monsieur Gadal took me to the Bethlehem Cave which is now closed, and he has begun the cleaning up preparatory to excavating. He has already found on the plateau [i.e. in the open, some distance from Bethlehem itself] a beautiful granite table with three massive granite supports—and this he has set up—it took five men to move it—and it looks most imposing. He has also found the carefully concealed entrance to an underground passage, which he has covered again for exploration later. Digging alone of course, he got away a lot of the earth from under the big stone in the cave and he has laid bare the keystone of a vault which must be a crypt under the floor level of the cave. This of course we must excavate. But the most marvellous thing is that in shifting this earth he came upon an enormous vase—18 inches or so high—carved as he thinks from a stalactite. It will have to be thoroughly cleaned before we can be certain about it. Well, today I was underneath that big stone which rests at both ends on solid masonry—and it is flat and polished underneath. There is a cavity immediately below in which the vase was found and below that masonry again, though forming what we don't know yet. (W.B. to his family, 20 May 1938.)

Unfortunately for Walter, further excavation at Bethlehem was not undertaken until after he had returned to England. The results were disappointing. Assisted by Karl Rinderknecht, a young Swiss enthusiast, Gadal had dug in the hope of uncovering the 'crypt under the floor level' but found nothing save solid rock. Excavations in the other caves were equally unsuccessful and nothing of note was found until the summer of 1939 when Gadal—again excavating alone—discovered two Egyptian Ushabti figures in a small cavity near the cave of l'Ermite.

By one of those amazing coincidences that often occur in the course of esoteric research, the two figures were strikingly similar to the two Ushabti that Walter had obtained during a winter holiday in Egypt and given to Gadal on his return to Ussat in May 1939, and by the operation of some unknown but immutable law the two pairs of figures had merged, unseen by human eye, into one.

With all these remarkable finds—the dove, the Grail, and the Egyptian god forms—Gadal may well have felt that the material treasure of Montségur had now been found, but there remained something more. All his work, whether conscious or unconscious, was to one end: the perpetuation of the continuing Cathar tradition in which he believed implicitly. This tradition was passed on from generation to generation and just as he had succeeded Garrigou (albeit with a variant title: to the local population he was known as 'The Cathar Pope') so another must succeed him. And the question of a successor had become urgent, for war was imminent and all work at Ussat would inevitably come to an end for its duration.

The formal ceremony took place on 16 September, the day before Walter's return to England, and was recorded in his diary perfunctorily and without comment: 'Gadal initiated Rind[erknecht] and me at Bethlehem, & formally passed me succession.' Karl Rinderknecht gave his own account of the occasion many years later in a letter to Walter: 'Mr. Gadal asked us to come to his house after supper. We followed him up the path to the rock-church of Ornolac, called Bethlehem. Entering the chapel we stood, in front of the pentacle, around the stone table (of Druidic origin?), Gadal in the centre, facing the pentacle, you on one side and I on the other. Gadal took one hand of each of us, placed it on the table and, after a moment of silence, he said, "The Patriarch of the Sabarthès, Adolphe Garrigou, himself initiated one hundred years ago, entrusted to me the safeguarding of the Cathar wisdom, the faith which he himself had received from predecessors. Since the world's destiny is in danger I wish to transmit this wisdom and faith to the disciples who have come with me here."'

Thus for Gadal the treasure of Montségur was not important—he had suffered, as we shall see, from the attentions of those who thought it was the Holy Grail and from the activities of those who believed it was bullion. All that mattered was that the doctrines of the Cathars and their high spirituality should be preserved. By initiating his successor he had, as he thought, guaranteed their survival. But the continuing pressures of war and isolation from those who believed as he did gave birth to doubts, and we shall also see how events in the post-war world led to his making strenuous efforts to ensure the continuance of the Cathar patriarchate in another direction. The appointment of a successor in 1939 was not the end of M. Gadal's life work.

4

Roché

DURING the 1930s Antonin Gadal may well have been the 'Cathar Pope'[1] to the people of Ussat, but to the academic world there was only one authority on Catharism who was both native to the Languedoc and a scholar: Déodat Roché, a lawyer of Castelnaudary in the Department of Aude, who held public office as Judge-President of the Assize Courts at Béziers. In May 1937 M. Roché delivered a paper on Catharism at the Congress of French Historians held at Montpellier. It was extremely well received and he was encouraged to revise and publish it (*Le Catharisme*, Toulouse, 1947; further revised and extended, Narbonne, 1973). His subsequent reputation as an historian of the Cathars is founded upon this work. He had previously written extensively on Catharism, but all of his early writings were unknown to the academic world as they had appeared in *Revue de la Science Spirituelle*, a journal dedicated to the promotion of the ideas of Rudolf Steiner. Not only was M. Roché a Cathar enthusiast, he was also a keen Anthroposophist, lecturing frequently at the Goetheanum (Steiner's extraordinary creation at Dornach in Switzerland, designed to be the headquarters of the Anthroposophical movement).

But for all his commitment to esoteric ideas, Roché did not believe himself to be a reborn Cathar and did not see himself as any kind of Master. Indeed, he specifically stated, in the course of a long letter to *la Dépêche de Toulouse* of 2 July 1939 that he had no wish to create a neo-Cathar movement and did not approach the subject as a believer, but rather as an historian and philosopher who 'studies the traces of the Gnostics, Manichees and Cathars in order to find in them the basis of modern spiritual science'.

And although he looked upon the caves of Ussat-Ornolac as an essential and most important part of the Cathar heritage, he did not look upon Gadal as a Cathar patriarch. He was, however, on friendly terms with him and often brought parties of Anthroposophists to visit the caves. On one of these visits Gadal introduced him to Walter, who recorded his impressions in a letter to his family (8 September 1938). Roché struck him as 'immensely learned, and at the same time modest and humble, though treated with great respect and even deference by those who accompanied him.' Gadal had previously told him that 'he thought M. Roché was practically an Adept and that he would in all probability be our chief later on'—an opinion that Gadal subsequently altered as he came to feel that 'M. Déodat Roché and his friends are inclining terribly to Anthroposophy and Dornach' (Gadal to Rinder-knecht, 14 September 1955). Walter, meanwhile, was somewhat surprised to find that 'the impression of power, which I would have expected, seemed to be completely lacking. Certainly he was tired and not too well, which may account for that. He was more like a modest and retiring old professor than anything else.' Above all, Walter was struck by Roché's gentleness and by his wish—quite unlike that of the average occultist— to share the fruits of his research.

Roché's researches were based upon his beliefs, which were somewhat strange. He believed that Mani, the Persian founder of Manichaeism, had given the Christ-impulse to Mithraism and that in this way Christianity had absorbed the spiritual essence of its great rival. It followed that when Manichaean dualist doctrines were brought to southern France by Bogomil missionaries in the tenth and eleventh centuries, the Languedocian dualists—the Cathars—utilized pre-existing Mithraic symbolism for the expression of their doctrines.

He was also a firm believer in a Mithraic presence at Ussat. Both in his book *Le Catharisme* and in a number of articles, Roché described the figure of Mithras, complete with Phrygian cap and surrounded by the sacred animals of Mithraism (the bull, serpent, dog and horse), that could be seen drawn upon the surface of the Pentagon in the Bethlehem cave. It did not, however, occur to him that what he saw— *'La figure de Mithra, coiffé du bonnet phrygien, y est tracée au manganèse'*— might have been natural markings in the limestone. When I visited the cave myself in 1983, nothing remotely like a figure of Mithras was visible, either on the Pentagon or anywhere else.

But for all its significance Ussat was not the most important Cathar site for Roché, nor, surprisingly, was Montségur. That honour was reserved for the ruined castle of Montréalp-de-Sos, which hangs upon the cliffs above the village of Vicdessos, not far from Ussat. Here, in the summer of 1932, the *Président du Syndicat d'Initiative* of Tarascon (and thus, in a sense, a rival of Gadal), Joseph Mandement and two of his friends, discovered a remarkable painting on the wall of a small cave beneath one of the castle's towers. Mandement described the painting in *la Dépêche* (quoted in Bernadac, *Le Mystère Otto Rahn*, p. 221, translation by RG): 'Five red crosses and a sixth, also red but apart from them, a red lance, a red hammer [*'marteau rouge'*—in fact it is difficult to understand how this object can be seen as anything other than a sword, which is how Roché interpreted it, RG], a disc (which perhaps represents a host or the Holy Spirit) surrounded by a crown of thorns, and lastly, underneath, a large rectangle decorated with crosses and six red tongues of fire [these are usually taken to be drops of blood, RG]. This represents the ark (or tabernacle) of the Graal. The whole of the right side of the wall is covered with a calcareous deposit and one assumes that the missing instruments, 'the sponge and the scourge', were shown on that side.'

When Roché was shown the painting he recognized it as being identical with an illustration found in a manuscript of the thirteenth century, la Queste del Saint Graal edited by Albert Pauphilet (Paris, 1923); and whereas Mandement had seen in this 'Blazon of the Knights of the Graal' all the instruments of the Passion, Roché saw a sword rather than a hammer, and a sun-disc rather than a host. He also saw clear signs that the painting had been made over Mithraic reliefs, including a raven and the head of Mithras wearing a Phrygian cap. From this Roché deduced that the castle had been the home of a secret knightly Order closely related to the Cathars and, as the treasure of Montségur had been brought to the Sabarthès, this must have been its resting place. The castle was none other than Montsalvat, the true Castle of the Grail, and the treasure was the Holy Grail itself.

If there had ever been a material cup it mattered little to Roché. For him the treasure was less concrete; in true Anthroposophical fashion he perceived it as a spiritual current that had flowed through every manifestation of the Mysteries of the West from the Druids and the priests of Mithras, to the Cathars and Templars, and on to the revelations of Rudolf Steiner at the present day. But for all his Mithraic obsessions Roché remained a scholar rather than an occultist and he went on to found, in 1949, the scholarly review Cahiers d'Etudes Cathares. This was not restricted, as one might have expected, to papers supporting Roché's ideas but was open, as it still is, to all academic studies of Catharism and related topics irrespective of the author's point of view. It is also a more appropriate memorial to Roché than the rock-painting of Montrealp-de-Sos: future generations of neo-Cathars may read the Cahiers at will, but the Graal Blazon, whatever its origin and significance, they cannot see, for in the fifty years since its discovery it has faded almost to the point of invisibility. The day of Mithras has evidently passed.

Roché was not alone in locating the Grail Castle in the Pyrenees, although those who believed that the Cathar treasure was the Holy Grail tended to identify Montségur with Montsalvat, and some of them expected to find the treasure hidden there even if they did not expect it to be in the form of a sacred vessel.

In September 1931 a M. Arnaud, an engineer working on hydro-electric projects in the Ariège region, announced that he had discovered a blocked-up cave entrance, behind rocks just below the walls of the castle, and that he confidently anticipated blasting his way through this obstruction to enter the subterranean passages and vaults that lay beyond it.[2] Within the vaults he was sure that he would find the treasure—not as the Grail cup but as the text of the secret Cathar version of the Gospel of John: publication of this Secret Gospel would lead inevitably to 'the realization of the Albigensian ideal, the Church of the Holy Spirit' (quoted in A. E. Waite, *The Holy Grail*, 1933, p. 560). Fortunately for the well-being of Montségur, M. Arnaud never carried out his dynamiting, but had he done so he would have found no passages and thus neither Gospel nor Grail.

In the early 1960s the whole of the Pog—the rock on which the castle of Montségur is built—was systematically studied by the *Société Spéléologique de l'Ariège*, whose members explored every natural cave and opening in the rock, finding not the slightest trace of the vast underground caverns described by Napoléon Peyrat and frantically sought by his credulous successors. One of the explorers, Fernand Niel, also studied the castle itself and argued that its significance was undeniably religious rather than military.[3] He pointed out that the original structure was not laid out for military use and that later alterations had no military significance. In 1204, when there was no reason to suppose that it would be needed as anything other than a place of worship (it was not garrisoned as a fort until 1232), the castle had been restored by Ramon de Perella at the Cathars' request. The whole plan of the castle, the measurements and angles of the walls and the precise positioning of specific features, indicates that it was astronomically aligned, and M. Niel concluded that the castle is really a sun temple carefully camouflaged as a fort. It is possible to observe sunrise from Montségur on every day of the year, and the castle, so M. Niel maintained, was specifically constructed so that the position of the rising sun could be fixed throughout the year.

He was also quite sure that the Cathar treasure had been taken out of Montségur on the night of 15 March 1244, and to prove—against those who doubted the possibility—that it could have been carried down the cliffs he climbed down them himself, following the route of Amiel Aicard. That it was taken to caves in the Sabarthès he had little doubt, but he was unsure as to its nature: perhaps it consisted of parchments on which were written the secrets of the Cathar religion, perhaps it was something else. Whatever it might have been, it was certainly something infinitely precious to the Cathars, whether or not it would have been desirable to ordinary mortals.

Other seekers were more mundane than either Niel or Arnaud.

One of them, a somewhat disreputable American named Wolff, came to Ussat with the avowed intention of profiting from the Cathars: if he could not find their treasure he would exploit their remains and make his fortune in that way.

Wolff pestered Gadal with ideas for exploiting the caves—even suggesting that they build a café on the terrace in front of the Bethlehem cave—but never made any real attempt to put his ideas into practice and spent his time drinking and upsetting the local population. Gadal had long recognized Wolff for the fool that he was and found him merely amusing, but the locals were more suspicious. They interpreted his American accent as German[4] and were convinced that he was a spy. His principal reason for staying in Ussat was, however, a desire to benefit from the treasure he was sure that Gadal either had found or was about to find.

When Walter met Wolff his initial reaction was one of dislike—to the extent of finding him 'positively repulsive and evil'[5]—and concern that he would disrupt work on the caves. These fears proved groundless, for Gadal was more than a match for Wolff.

On the one occasion that Wolff made a determined effort at excavation,

Gadal wouldn't let him touch Bethlehem so he put him on to a remote cave which has been blocked up and needs opening. Wolff meanwhile had sent for a man to come from Paris and help him—all at his expense (Wolff's). Then Gadal took them to the cave and I went to see the fun. It was the toughest you could pick. Can you imagine Wolff clambering along a ledge overlooking a precipice and climbing through thorn bushes etc.! He puffed and sweated and swore like a trooper. At every step he got into a worse and worse temper and finally when he got tired of carrying the pick-axe which got in his way he threw it over the cliff! By the time we got to the cave he had had enough so he left his tools and went back for a drink. Since then he has been resting—and drinking aperitifs—and his man kicks his heels at Wolff's expense. Gadal says he has always been like that. A terrific lot of talk about what he is going to do—and then after a day or two when he finds it hard work he chucks it. I asked Gadal what on earth makes him do it—and he said he was always hoping to find buried treasure—but it had to be easy—just crack open a rock with a pick and pouf! The cave of Ali-Baba all complete! (WB to family, 28 July 1938.)

After this escapade Walter revised his opinion of Wolff and saw him as 'just a chump who thinks he can get rich quickly'. The authorities, however, were less tolerant, eventually taking such exception to Wolff's activities (he was 'usually surrounded by suspicious looking German and Spanish refugees') that he was obliged to leave Ussat: 'Wolff left on Thursday, to everybody's great relief. He has become absolutely impossible. He thinks of nothing but his aperitif and his dogs,[6] and spends his whole time drinking and running down everybody and everything, and to cap it all he began to parade a scandalous affair with a woman of doubtful reputation. The natives are all convinced he is a spy, and he certainly interests himself overmuch in Spanish refugees.' (WB to family, 4 September 1938.)

Wolff was clearly not a man in the Cathar mould, but he had the misfortune to possess a German name and the people of Ussat immediately assumed that he was in some way connected with another seeker after the Grail who most certainly *was* German and who as certainly did not endear himself to them.

This was Otto Rahn (1904–39), a young German scholar who had become fascinated by the Grail legend through his love of Wagner and especially of his *Parsifal*. Rahn intended to write a dissertation on Kyot, or Guyot, the Provençal troubadour on whose lost Grail poem Wolfram von Eschenbach claimed to have based his *Parzival*, and in 1931 he came to the Languedoc to look for the original of the Grail castle which was supposed to be in either Southern France or Northern Spain. (Wolfram states that Kyot's poem utilized an Arabic manuscript found in Toledo, and Wagner set *his* Grail castle in the Pyrenees.) It is almost certain that Rahn already saw Montségur as Montsalvat and looked upon the Grail as the Cathar treasure, for he would have been familiar with Joséphin Péladan's *Le Secret des Troubadours* (Paris, 1906) in which the identification of the Cathars with the Grail Knights and of Montségur with the castle of the Grail was first made. Knowing too where the treasure had been taken, he decided to settle at Ussat in order to explore the caves of the Sabarthez.

Gadal was delighted: here at last was a real enthusiast who appreciated the importance of the caves. He expounded his theories to Rahn and gave him the freedom of his library and of his private museum. Rahn, in his turn, was deeply impressed—both by Gadal, whom he called his 'Trevrizent' (the uncle of Parsifal in Wolfram's text), and by the concept of the caves of Initiation as set out in Gadal's *Au Chemin du Saint Graal*.[7] His own ideas developed rapidly and he began to sketch out the plan of the book that he hoped would launch him on his literary career.

In order to pursue his researches, however, he needed money, and in May 1932 he took out a lease on the Hotel des Marronniers at Ussat to provide himself with an income. But, as was almost inevitably the case with these dreamers who sought the Grail, he proved to be utterly incompetent as a businessman and by September he was hopelessly in debt. To escape his creditors—he owed money to his staff, to his landlord, and to his suppliers—he fled first from Ussat and then from France: not quite the behaviour one would expect from such an ardent admirer of Cathar morality.

Back in Germany he continued to correspond with Gadal and arranged to have his completed manuscript published. The book, *Kreuzzug gegen den Gral*, appeared in 1933 and in the following year a French translation, *La Croisade contre le Graal*, was issued. Academic critics dismissed Rahn's thesis, the book was not well received, and a proposed English version was never published. It did, however, gain acceptance among one very influential group of readers and it was that very acceptance that was to lead, in time, to the most fantastic speculations about Rahn's career and about his real purpose in visiting Ussat.

Rahn maintained—against all evidence and all scholarly opinion— that hidden within the Grail Romances was the essence of Catharism. The Quest of the Holy Grail was a symbolic presentation of Cathar initiation and the Grail itself (which in Wolfram's *Parzival* is a sacred stone) symbolized the Secret Doctrine of the Cathars. Wolfram's text is necessarily the only one of significance, deriving as it does from the Cathar-inspired Kyot, and all the features of *Parzival* have a true interpretation in Cathar terms.

To support this curious theory, which he expanded to include the extravagant claim that the Cathars derived from the Druids, Rahn pointed out what he saw as distinctive Cathar elements in the Parzival story. The hermit whom Parzival visits on his way to the Grail castle eats no meat and must, therefore, be a Cathar, while his cave of Fontane must be Fontanet in the Sabarthès and its natural altar a particularly striking stalagmite which can be seen in that cave. The initiation of Parzival by Trevrizent involves the giving of a robe and is thus a symbol of the Cathar rite of the Consolamentum, while the Castle of the Grail, Montsalvat, is evidently Montségur. And if further proof were needed, Montségur was originally a sanctuary of Belissena, the Druidic moon goddess, who is also Artemis to whom the dove— the Cathar symbol of the Holy Spirit—is sacred.

Within the Grail castle Parzival is shown the Holy Grail—the *lapis exilis,* or, *lapis ex coelis,* the stone fallen from heaven that is the shining stone, the Desire of Paradise. This stone was to be identified, according to Rahn, with the Mani stone of Buddhism—itself fallen from heaven—for were not the Cathars, when not deriving from the Druids, derived from the Persian Mani-chees?

Nor did his tortuous reasoning and linguistic lunacy end here. Rahn also claimed that the Holy Grail, the shining stone, was a real object and that it was the true treasure that was smuggled out of Montségur before its fall. This most holy relic was then hidden in the caves of the Sabarthès where it yet awaits discovery.

Given Rahn's theory it seems obvious that he stayed at Ussat simply to seek the Grail, but to some his presence was later seen as part of an obscure Nazi plot. Precisely what this plot was has never been made clear, and there is no evidence at all to show that the Nazi hierarchy had any significant interest in the Cathars or in Montségur.[8] Rahn's Grail fantasy, with its undertones of a Celtic and Nordic struggle against Latin Christianity, did, however, harmonize with Nazi racial philosophy and it was almost inevitable that Rahn would join the Nazi party. In 1936 he entered the SS and by 1938 he held the rank of Obersturmfuhrer (Lieutenant). But he was never to return to France, for on 13 March 1939—almost on the anniversary of the fall of Montségur —he lost his life in a snow-storm in the Tyrolean Alps.

Recent amateur historians of neo-Catharism, notably Christian Bernadac, have denied that Rahn died in 1939 and have claimed that he was really Rudolf Rahn, the German ambassador to Italy in 1943, that he was 'controlled' at Ussat by Wolff, who was in reality Karl Wolff, the SS general who negotiated the German surrender in Italy in 1945, and that both men went on to work for the Americans. There is, of course, not the slightest evidence to justify these claims and faced with such lunacy it is something of a relief to return to Gadal and his search for the real treasure of Montségur.

5

From Gadal to Galaad

EARLY in 1949 Déodat Roché founded his journal *Cathiers d'Etudes Cathares*—taking as its symbol the figure of a dove found at Ornolac[1]—and in July of that year he took the delegates to the second 'Congrès d'Etudes Cathares' on a tour of Cathar sites. At Montréalp-de-Sos they saw the Grail Blazon and heard Roché lecture on the Pyrenean Grail; at Ussat-les-Bains they explored the Cavern of Lombrives, and at Montségur they listened to a stirring poem in Occitan on Esclarmonde de Pereille, the heroine of the siege who had been burned with her fellow Cathars when the castle fell. Gadal took no part in all this as he was busy with the more important task of restoring to public view the lost glories of the caves of Ornolac.

It was proving to be an increasingly difficult task. After the end of the Second World War Walter Birks had returned to Ussat where he and Gadal attempted to revive the fortunes of the Spa and the Hotel des Bains; but post-war austerity did not encourage tourism and this, coupled with financial constraints, denied them success so that in 1948 the lease was given up. Walter, who was by this time becoming increasingly disenchanted with all esoteric approaches to the problem of the Cathars, took up his teaching career in the Middle East and the promotion of Ussat-les-Bains as the epicentre of Catharism was left entirely in the hands of Gadal. There it remained until 1955 and the arrival of a new body of enthusiasts from the Netherlands.

The descent of this army of some hundreds of eager neo-Cathars—members of the Young Gnostic Brotherhood accompanied by their two Grand Masters— was viewed with mixed feelings by the people of Ussat, who were secretly rather proud of Gadal and unwilling to see his work absorbed into that of a large, unknown, and foreign 'Brotherhood'. But absorbed it was, and the absorption took concrete form on 5 May 1957 with the unveiling of the 'Monument Galaad'. According to the Young Gnostics, this monument (which essentially comprises a replica of the 'altar table' from Bethlehem—a large flat stone supported by three smaller round stones, mounted on a cubical plinth and surrounded by a circle of twelve granite standing stones) 'represents the visible connection in space and time, of the labour of the Tribune of the Light "the Brotherhood of the Holy Grail", "The Brotherhood of the Cathars", "the Brotherhood of the Rosycross". It is the covenant of the active Christ-Hierarchy, which has carried out the work of harvesting during the past two thousand years in the western world.'[2] As for the name, 'Galaad means "The Stone of the Witness", it is the visible token of the covenant between the two links of the Universal Chain of Brotherhoods.'[3]

Others saw it in a different light. In his book on Otto Rahn, Christian Bernadac denounced the Dutch Rosicrucians bitterly: 'Gadal, alone, abandoned, with not the slightest hope of pupil or successor, fell into the hands of those who wanted to find"proofs" for their speculative charlatanism (with so little true spirituality), who pretended to believe in him in order to exploit his discoveries. Gadal, who made Ussat-les-Bains and its caves known to the whole world, even if he was sometimes mistaken in mixing poetic dreams and legends with history, deserves better than this heap of stones—a memorial born of the delirium of the new worshippers of obscurantism.'[4]

All of which was, to say the least, a little unkind. The Young Gnostic Brotherhood was one aspect of the work of the Lectorium Rosicrucianum, which had been founded at Haarlem in the Netherlands in 1952 by J. van Rijckenborgh and Catharose da Petri. Its aim was to make known 'the Septuple World-Brotherhood of the Golden Rosycross', and van Rijckenborgh defined the movement when he answered the question 'What is the Brotherhood?' at a conference at Wiesbaden in September 1952.

The Brotherhood is the unity of the well-disposed, the communion of the children of God. All those who through the opened rose-heart enter into the manifested new radiation-field, are linked into the chain of the Brotherhood. The force of this bond is determined by ourselves, by our own state-of-being and there is nobody who is able to prevent your adoption by the Brotherhood, unless you stand in your own way. Now that you know the purpose of the Fama [i,e, the *Fama Fraternitatis,* one of the original Rosicrucian manifestoes of the early seventeenth century] it is necessary to discuss its character. If the aim is a decision upon a direct new attitude towards life by all who can and will make such a decision, the character of the Fama is to give information with regard to the why and wherefore. Well then, we have to understand what is coming to pass in these years; what is coming to the fore.

There is an electro-magnetic radiation-field of the Christ-Hierophants and some people in this fallen world have learned to react upon it with the open rose-heart. They live in all parts of our world; in all countries these brothers and sisters are to be found .They have learned to react upon the electro-magnetic radiations of the Brotherhood.[5]

Such pronouncements, which undoubtedly seem extraordinary if not quite incomprehensible to the uninitiated, led Bernadac (who already mistrusted all neo-Cathars) to conceive an extreme distaste for the Lectorium Rosicrucianum and for its leaders. This distaste blinded him to the transparent sincerity of both 'Grand Masters' and he failed to recognize that far from exploiting Gadal, they brought with them international recognition—albeit within strictly esoteric circles—of the importance of his discoveries.

Gadal himself was delighted at their coming, but it was not his work alone that had brought them to Ussat-les-Bains. Van Rijckenborgh and his companions believed that the valley of the Ariège held a special spiritual significance, for they maintained that the Cathars were the spiritual forerunners of the Rosicrucians, and they were convinced—as were the Polaires—that Christian Rosencreutz had visited the castle of Lordat on his way home from Spain to Germany. Lordat, however, was difficult of access and Ussat-les-Bains, with its caves of Cathar initiation, proved to be the ideal place for the building of a centre from which the spiritual regeneration of mankind could radiate.

The monument was merely the beginning. In August 1958 the Galaad Centre at Ussat-les-Bains was officially opened and Gadal's 'old dream' began to come true. Visiting Rosicrucians would find not only a lecture theatre, but 'a refectory, kitchens, men's and women's dormitories, sick-bay—for 250 to 300 people. A private camping site which I have opened for 150 people, will permit a great increase in numbers of visitors.' (Gadal to Rinderknecht, 19 July 1958.)

For Gadal it was important that the centre should be for the sowing of knowledge and not for the harvesting of money. He had become convinced that Roché, the gradual diminution of whose following he attributed to Roché's obsessive concern with Anthroposophy, was selling out to Mammon: 'The misfortune is he has let himself be taken in to organize a Cathar Congress and set up a Cathar museum. I have sent nothing [to the museum] I don't accept it. . . . I hope, with the help of the Dutch R +C to set up in a Museum the great quantity of things found in the caves. Naturally the takings at the Cathar Museum at Castres has produced a lot of money. Soon we shall change that "Golden Calf".' (Gadal to Rinderknecht, 14 September 1955.)

With the development of the centre at Ussat-les-Bains the museum became a reality and Gadal enthused about it: 'I must tell you I have built a museum; everything I have found in our caves from speleology and geology to medieval history. Many learned visitors both, civil and religious, have found it good and well set-up.' (Gadal to Rinderknecht, 19 July 1958).

Nor was this all, for Gadal himself was now travelling about Europe propagating his personal version of Cathar doctrines—'sowing the good seed of Pyrenean Catharism', as he put it—among the assembled faithful in Germany, Switzerland, and the Netherlands. And for those who could not hear him in person there was a new edition of his book *Sur le Chemin du Saint-Graal* (Haarlem, 1960), illustrated with views of the Symbolic Wall, the Mystic Gate, the Galaad Centre, and the Monument. Perhaps because no one within it reacted 'with the opened rose-heart' the English-speaking world was curiously neglected: Gadal never visited Britain and no account of his work was available in English until 1981. Even then only a brief guide to Bethlehem and Lombrives, with descriptions of the Musée Gadal and of the Monument, was issued. English neo-Cathars have not followed the way of the Holy Grail.

Nor have the inhabitants of the Ariège, for while Gadal continued to spread his Cathar Gospel to the nations, the people of Ussat-les-Bains remained stubbornly indifferent both to native Catharism and to imported Rosicrucianism, and the Young Gnostic Brotherhood made few local converts. After Gadal's death in 1962 the absence of local support led to difficulties in maintaining the Galaad Centre, and in 1968 the buildings were sold and have been used ever since as holiday homes for children.

The Musée Gadal was moved to a new home at Tarascon while the Monument remained at Ussat-les-Bains—to be visited every year by members of the still thriving Lectorium Rosicrucianum, who come to seek their version of the Cathar treasure in the caves of Ornolac. Whether or not they find it, they are living proof that Gadal's dreams did not die with him and a memorial to his work, for if the Cathars were not in evidence at Ussat in the days of Crusade and Inquisition, they most certainly are now.

6

The Treasure That Never Was

THE combination of the work of the Lectorium Rosicrucianum and a growing, latterday Languedocian nationalism has ensured the survival of neo-Catharism in Southern France, but in England—where dualism never took root as a philosophical creed—it has never captured the popular imagination. It did, however, stir that imagination in 1970 when a somewhat sensational book, *The Cathars and Reincarnation*, offered a novel approach to the study of Cathar history and belief. Medievalists and Church historians had always been familiar with the events of the Albigensian Crusade and with the nature of the allegedly heretical beliefs that led to it, but neither the intelligent layman nor the committed occultist had shown much enthusiasm for what they saw as an obscure episode of French history. Dr Guirdham's book undoubtedly altered that perception.

Arthur Guirdham is a retired psychiatrist who had been senior consultant in psychiatry to the Bath clinical area, and thus a man presumed to be both scholarly and objective in his approach to the subject matter of his book. He was, and still is, however, an enthusiast for, and believer in, extrasensory elements in the healing of psychiatric illnesses, writing extensively on his interests. Laudable though this enthusiasm may be, it seems to have overridden objectivity when Dr Guirdham came to deal with the Cathars.

The educated reader of *The Cathars and Reincarnation*, and of the author's other works on the Cathars, feels decidedly uneasy when he encounters such statements as: 'There is no reasonably full and informative history of Catharism known to me in English' (*op. cit.*, p. 199), or 'when [in 1944] not more than a handful of beings in this country can have known even the broadest outlines of Cathar ritual' (*Catharism: the Medieval Resurgence of Primitive Christianity*, 1969, p. 21). These statements are simply untrue; Dr Guirdham may be excused for being ignorant of S. R. Maitland's *Facts and Documents Illustrative of the History, Doctrine, and Rites of the Ancient Albigenses and Waldenses* (1838),

THE TREASURE OF MONTSÉGUR

but it is difficult to believe that a true scholar would not have known of H. J. Warner's *The Albigensian Heresy* (2 vols., 1922, 1928), a book widely praised (and widely read) and reprinted in 1979.

In a later book, *The Great Heresy* (1977), unease turns to a suspicion of special pleading: Dr Guirdham ignores the recently published *Heresy, Crusade and Inquisition in Southern France, 1100–1250* (1974) by W. L. Wakefield, and refers the reader instead to Edmond Holmes's *The Holy Heretics* (1948), on the grounds that this superficial and virulently anti-Catholic work is 'intuitive but sober'. Of contemporary French authorities on the Cathars he selects only Nelli, Duvernoy, and Roché for mention, ignoring the equally authoritative Yves Dossat and Christine Thouzellier, whose views go decidedly against those espoused by Dr Guirdham. All this is not to labour a point but to indicate the level of objectivity—rather the utter lack of it—in Dr Guirdham's approach to the study of Catharism.

Unlike academic historians, Dr Guirdham does not rely on contemporary documents for his knowledge of the Cathars, but uses them merely to verify information obtained from a rather different source: 'You might ask me where I get this information. There is in these days a considerable literature on the subject, and there are also the Inquisitorial records. But in actual fact I have other sources. I have been directly rather than scholastically informed in the course of medical practice.' (*Catharism*, p. 19.)

That direct information came from the members of a group of thirteenth-century Cathar Perfecti who had reincarnated, more or less at the same time, in the twentieth century and who came together in the 1960s. Conveniently, they all lived in the neighbourhood of Bath. Dr Guirdham's initial informant was a patient, whom he calls Mrs Smith, who was referred to him in 1962 suffering from a recurring nightmare; this, he discovered, was her reliving in sleep of the persecution of her former thirteenth-century self. Even more startling was his discovery that he himself had been closely linked to Mrs Smith in his own previous life as a Cathar. This story was told in *The Cathars and Reincarnation*, while the gradual mutual recognition of other members of the group, and the subsequent research into their past lives, was related in *We are One Another* (1974). Finally Dr Guirdham issued a study of Cathar history and beliefs, *The Great Heresy* (1977), in which 'the deeper teachings' of Catharism, 'communicated by a group of discarnate entities', are revealed. Being received at first hand these are—as might be expected—at once more detailed and more reliable than any description of Cathar ideas derived from documentary sources by conventional historians. Not surprisingly they also support both Dr Guirdham's personal beliefs and his own, highly idiosyncratic view that 'Catharism was the reappearance in the twelfth and

thirteenth centuries of the religion of emanation and psychic communication which we call Christianity but which was modified
beyond all recognition from the third century onwards' (*Catharism*,
p. 19).

Given this unworldly attitude to Catharism it is only to be expected
that the Cathar treasure is of less significance for Dr Guirdham than
the revelations of discarnate Cathars on transmigration, auras,
mechanisms of evil (used by the inquisitors, of course), and future
lives on other planets ('the psyche, escaped from matter, actually
moves towards the planet best adapted to its system of vibration': not
content with doing violence to history, Dr Guirdham does violence to
astronomy also). Nevertheless, many of the reincarnated Cathars had
died at Montségur and Dr Guirdham discusses the treasure more than
once.

He rejects the idea that it might have been a sacred chalice: 'A faith
which did not build churches, rejected sacraments, and was uninterested
in holy relics was not likely to have concerned itself with an object
of this nature.' (*Great Heresy*, p. 85.) But it is still a material treasure, and
one of his reborn Cathars (Miss Mills) identified it for him by means
of her automatic writing: 'Treasure—No. Books—Yes.' (*We are One
Another*, p. 33.) Later, in *The Great Heresy*, he enlarges on the nature of
these books; not only were some of them lost Gospels, but they
included 'a collection of rare but not necessarily unique books. These
included the works of Greek philosophers from Pythagoras to Plato.
Democritus and Epicurus were among their number. The neo-
Platonists and, in particular, Plotinus and Porphyry were well represented. So were the Alexandrine School. The works of Valentinus
and Basilides were included in the Cathar library' (p. 86). Even more
important were the 'frankly esoteric communications' of 'two or three
of the Parfaits who had delved deep into philosophy by means of what
I suppose would now be called transcendental meditation, committed
to parchment what they had seen and experienced and knew to be
true. Guilhabert de Castres [one of the discarnate entities] certainly
wrote a record of the basic and undeviating truths which he had
experienced' (p. 85). He did not, however, tell Dr Guirdham just how
the four escapees carried this library on their backs down the sheer
cliffs of Montségur.

Thus for English neo-Cathars of the reincarnation school the
treasure was a record of occult truths. But as transmitted by Dr
Guirdham they bear an amazing similarity to the very Victorian occult
truths handed down to posterity by the Mahatmas of Madame
Blavatsky, and their immediate source may be more prosaic than the
discarnate Cathars who surround Dr Guirdham. Throughout the
1920s and early 1930s a Dr Thomas Penry-Evans held a senior post at

Charing Cross Hospital; he also spent much time working with his wife—Dion Fortune—to develop their magical order, The Fraternity of the Inner Light, the concerns of which included the recall of past lives. Senior members of the order are known to have recorded visions of past lives from the time of the Albigensian Crusade (complete with esoteric lore), and it seems likely that their associates were aware of these lives. Whether or not Dr Guirdham associated with them is not known, but given his interests he may well have met them for in 1929 he too was then working at Charing Cross Hospital. If this was so he may well have lost what he learned to his unconscious mind, only to draw it up again with no knowledge of its source forty years later.

This is, of course, pure speculation, but whatever the source of Dr Guirdham's enthusiasm it was remarkably successful in bringing the Cathars to the attention of the English 'occult' public, leading, in due course, to their utilization by a trio of occult historians in an even more extraordinary way. For these people, however, the Cathars and their treasure were subordinate to an even greater treasure—that of Rennes-le-Chateau, a tiny village some twenty-five miles to the east of Montségur.

Rennes-le-Chateau is notable today for the ever-increasing number of tourists who come to marvel at the curious church built at the turn of the last century by the parish priest, Bérenger Saunière, and to seek further clues to the nature of the vast treasure Saunière is alleged to have found. In brief, Saunière is supposed to have uncovered an unidentified 'treasure' as a result of deciphering manuscripts that he found hidden in the church; whatever it was enabled him to obtain great wealth, to reconstruct the church in a somewhat bizarre fashion, and to build a curious tower, the Magdalene, in the village. French chroniclers of the tale—those, that is, who believe there *was* a treasure—tend to identify the treasure as the gold of the Templars or of the Merovingian kings of France, but the three principal English investigators of the suppositious mystery tell a different tale.

In their book *The Holy Blood and the Holy Grail* (1982), Michael Baigent, Richard Leigh, and Henry Lincoln argue that the treasure is knowledge of a great secret: nothing less than knowledge of the surviving bloodline of Jesus Christ, Who did not die upon the cross but fled to Southern France with Mary Magdalene and their children. The descendants of the family were then protected down the ages by a mysterious Order, the Prieuré de Sion, until Saunière discovered their secret and utilized his discovery to gain his wealth. To support this lunatic theory the three authors drag in—amidst an inchoate mass of irrelevancies—the Cathars and the treasure that was smuggled out of Montségur.

Like Dr Guirdham they reject the possibility that it was the Holy

Grail in the form of a chalice, but they also deny that the treasure was material at all: 'Could the Cathar "treasure", like the "treasure" Saunière discovered, have consisted primarily of a secret? Could that secret have been related, in some unimaginable way, to something that became known as the Holy Grail?' (*The Holy Blood and the Holy Grail*, p. 33). Nor are they sure that the 'treasure' was really 'taken to the fortified caves of Ornolac in the Ariège, where a band of Cathars was exterminated shortly after', but suggest instead that 'Whatever was smuggled out of Montségur might well have been brought to Rennes-le-Chateau, or, more likely, to one of the caves which honeycomb the surrounding mountains. And if the "secret" of Montségur was what Saunière subsequently discovered, that would obviously explain a great deal' (pp. 33–4).

If the treasure, or 'secret', *was* knowledge of the bloodline of Jesus it would explain the Cathar rejection of the cross, and also, if the Roman Church suspected the existence of the 'secret', explain both Crusade and Inquisition: 'Was it possible, in short, that the Cathars (or at least certain Cathars) knew something—something that contributed to the frenzied fervour with which Rome sought their extermination?' p. 34)

And so, by way of piling one unproven hypothesis upon another, the Cathar treasure has progressed (in England, at least) from Dr Guirdham's rare manuscripts of occult knowledge to the equally hidden knowledge of a married Jesus whose descendants yet live to threaten the very fabric of the Christian Church. One might hope that this folly represented the limit of esoteric speculation, but there are, alas, no bounds to the wild imaginings of occultists.

In the footsteps of the authors of *The Holy Blood and the Holy Grail*—but with far greater hope of emulating their critical failure than of repeating their commercial success—have come other English writers with their own theories about Rennes-le-Chateau, once again linking the treasure to the Cathars. Perhaps the most original of these are Patricia and Lionel Fanthorpe, who rebutted the bloodline theory in their book *The Holy Grail Revealed: The Real Secret of Rennes-le-Chateau* (1982). For them the treasure of Montségur, and thus of Rennes, is purely material and before its removal was first taken *into* the fortress: 'The thing could have been taken from the wall tomb at Rennes and smuggled up the hazardous cliffs of Montségur' (p. 140). Its arrival, however, proved unwelcome: *'the garrison leaders are horrified*. Knowing that Montségur must soon fall to the Catholic crusaders, the defenders' chief anxiety now is to get the secret out again and back to a place of safety where it will not fall into the hands of their enemies' (p. 140). Their horror is not surprising, for the 'treasure' is not only material, it is unearthly in the strict sense: it is, in fact, extra-terrestrial. Exactly what it is the Fanthorpes do not say, beyond suggesting that it produces infinite wealth, and they content themselves by concluding with a question: 'If the core of the treasure is a strange artifact, an inexplicable power source created by some ancient, long-forgotten technology, or brought to Earth in a starship, what can it do and where did it originate?' (p. 143)

An extra-terrestrial treasure might explain the Cathar interest in the descent of angelic beings into matter, but neither the Fanthorpes nor any other of the non-spiritual neo-Cathars seem to have considered that such a treasure most probably originated in the ever-fertile imagination of ordinary human beings.

Other theories and other theorists will doubtless arise for the question of the treasure of Montségur is of a type that proves perennially fascinating to human curiosity; but not one of the neo-Cathar seekers to date has understood the true nature of the treasure. It was not gold, nor yet the Holy Grail, the lost Gospel of John, the secret life of Jesus, or a nameless object from the stars; not one of the attempted explanations of its nature fits what is known of the Cathars, and thus what is likely to have been of such supreme importance for them. For fifty years neo-Cathars have failed to grasp the significance of the treasure; if we are to succeed where they have failed and to grasp the truth that has constantly eluded them, we must leave behind their alarms and diversions and turn to the Cathars as they were in reality. To know what the treasure was we must know what Catharism was and whence it came: we must know what the Cathars themselves believed and taught.

PART TWO

7

Catharism: The Historical Setting

FROM the break-up of the Roman Empire in the West in the fifth century until after the year 1000 the long night of the Dark Ages covered Western Europe. Barbarian invaders swept over the land, raiding and pillaging, or founding transient and fluctuating kingdoms. Ancient civilization, built upon secure city life and uninterrupted communications, succumbed, and a greatly depleted population was reduced once more to subsistence agriculture. Men clustered in rustic communities about the stronghold of some chieftain powerful enough to afford them protection in exchange for servitude. Life became narrow and parochial, and for the mass of mankind the intellectual and moral horizon shrank like the physical one to the fields from which a scanty and precarious livelihood had to be wrung.

During this long and sombre period society was held together by the Church, the one institution which remained stable and continuous. The Church impressed the barbarian conquerors with the majesty and dignity of Roman civilization and the Christian ideal of society. Thanks to it the chaos of the barbarian migrations was eventually reduced to the order and stability of medieval Christendom. But in accomplishing this great civilizing task the character of the Church itself was necessarily profoundly modified. Pomp and splendour were developed to impress the imagination of the barbarian, while the bishops and abbots, in becoming the mentors and guides of kings and chieftains, insensibly became worldly statesmen and feudal lords. An increasing part of their time and energy also came to be occupied in the stewardship of the wealth with which the Church was endowed by a pious and grateful laity. The Church had upheld in an age of chaos and darkness that the things of the spirit are greater than the material and the kingdom of God above the kingdoms of the world. But by its very success in imposing these conceptions the claim to the superiority of the spirit had insensibly become a claim to temporal domination by an institution, and the noble dream of a kingdom of Christ on Earth had become the ambition of the Pope to rule as a worldly monarch. The Church had saved Christian civilization at a heavy cost to its own spiritual integrity.

By the eleventh century life in Western Europe was becoming more stable and secure. The violent displacements of barbarian peoples had at last reached equilibrium and the gradual development of the feudal system was bringing some sort of order and security into daily life. And as soon as man began to be delivered, to some slight degree, from fear and from the oppressive daily problem of ensuring his mere animal existence, he began to discover his soul and become more conscious of his spiritual needs. When this happened a vast potential of religious vitality was found to be awaiting expression. This vitality first manifested itself in the increasing popularity of pilgrimages to the tombs of various saints and ultimately to the Holy Land. At the close of the eleventh century it reveals itself most strikingly in the overwhelming response to the preaching of the first Crusade. Besides the knights and nobles who constituted the armed force of the Crusade and whose doings are chiefly recorded by the historians, thousands of humble folk, driven by the impulsion of a barely understood emotional and unconscious spiritual need, set off under the guidance of Peter the Hermit and Walter the Penniless, and tramped in vast hordes through the Balkans to Byzantium. This spontaneous popular movement was a new thing in the history of the world. Not only was it a symptom of the immense latent spiritual energy which was blindly seeking expression, but it had far-reaching consequences in widening the intellectual horizon of Western Europe. As the survivors straggle back home from the Balkans and the Near East they will be found to carry many strange seeds which will germinate profusely in the awakening soul of twelfth-century Christendom.

For at the same time there was growing up a universal and vaguely formulated desire for a more intense and ardent inner life. This found expression in a number of enthusiastic popular movements of a revivalist character, in which three main currents may be discerned. There was first an appeal to a life of renunciation and voluntary poverty, which led inevitably to an attack on the wealth and political power of the contemporary Church. Secondly, there was an appeal to the authority of the Gospels and the direct inspiration of the Spirit, leading to criticism of all contemporary institutions contrary to their teaching. Thirdly, there was an undercurrent of Gnostic and Manichaean ideas derived from the Balkans, and characterized by a dualist explanation of the origin of evil.

Among the most widespread and enduring of these popular revivalist movements was that known as Waldensian or Vaudois. Peter Valdo, a rich citizen of Lyon, appalled at the ignorance of the masses, caused translations of the Gospels and some other parts of the Bible to be made in the vulgar tongue. About the year 1160 he distributed all his goods to the poor and gathered about himself a band of disciples, equally dedicated to poverty, who went about preaching. The Waldenses claimed to draw their teachings entirely from the Bible and in their origins were so far from rejecting the authority of the Church that a deputation of them went to Rome in 1179 to ask the Pope for official recognition of their movement. The Church, which at first had seemed to tolerate the movement, was however, changing its attitude and the Waldenses were forbidden to preach unless requested by the clergy. In 1184 the doctrines of those who 'falsely call themselves the humble or poor men of Lyon' were denounced in a Papal constitution, and they were associated with the Cathari and Paterini who, as we shall see, were a movement of very different origin, though having many external points of resemblance.

The Waldenses anticipated by half a century St Francis of Assisi and his Minor Brothers and, had the Church been more prescient and less obsessed by the importance of fine points of doctrine, it could perhaps have won this movement to its cause as it later did that of St Francis. The Waldenses preached absolute obedience to the commands of the Gospel, held that it was unlawful to swear an oath or to kill, and that obedience should be given only to good priests. Office and order are of no avail for consecrating or blessing, binding or loosing, where the priest is unworthy, and a good layman can equally well fulfil his functions. Transubstantiation takes place in the hand of him who worthily receives and the Host can be consecrated at an ordinary table. They said that prayers in Latin were profitless if the people did not understand them and they condemned infant baptism, prayers for the dead, Holy Orders, Extreme Unction, and the tonsure. They despised decretals, indulgences, excommunications, canonizations, relics, crosses, times and seasons—in brief, they preached that the doctrine of Christ and His Apostles was sufficient for salvation without the statutes of the Church. Their ideas spread widely, particularly into Southern France, Switzerland, and Piedmont. In Italy they came into contact with the similar ideas which had been propagated by Arnaldo of Brescia, and the Poor of Lyon fusing with the Poor of Lombardy survived, despite persecution, until absorbed by the Reformation.

These popular spiritual movements of the eleventh and twelfth centuries presented a perplexing problem to the Church, which was at first quite unprepared to meet them and incapable of comprehending or satisfying the urge that gave them birth. Historians have often failed to understand the real nature of the problem, tending instead to express themselves according to their individual bias. If Catholic, they see the Church called upon to defend itself against heretical doctrines subversive of society and true religion, even against the menace of Antichrist, while the anti-Catholic sees priestcraft defending its privileges and stamping ruthlessly upon the sparks of pure spirituality. The reality is not quite so simple and the difficulties may be better appreciated if we endeavour to place them in historical perspective.

On the one hand is the Roman Catholic Church which has piloted mankind through the long night of the Dark Ages, which has for seven centuries embodied the order and stability of human society, which sees itself as the law, the conscience, and the sole instructor and guide of a humanity darkened by ignorance and burdened by fear. How can it appreciate these stirrings of spiritual adolescence when it has long forgotten that mankind would ever grow up? On the other hand, although humanity is emerging from the Dark Ages, it is not yet ripe for the Reformation. Ignorance is still profound, and the urge which is driving men is still largely unconscious and uncomprehended. Man is blindly groping for a more intense spiritual life but his striving only too frequently finds expression in crude, hysterical, anti-social, and subversive forms. The more contemplative spirits, in whom the urge was for a more ardent inner life, could seek satisfaction in the recently re-formed monastic orders, but the extraverted masses demanded that this intenser spiritual life should be manifested in the established order of things. Yet in the twelfth century the Church *is* the established order of things, and at the same time the unique channel of spiritual life.

Inevitably, then, revivalist movements are led into criticism of the Church, and the Church on its part cannot tolerate that ignorant men should seek to replace its own well-tried standards by the aberrations of self-taught visionaries. Nor can it, at this stage of its development, revert to its infancy and a life of apostolic poverty, for it has become, as the result of its own priceless service to humanity in the Dark Ages, far too deeply interwoven in the very texture of the society it has nursed back to civilization. This is a dilemma which will eventually be resolved in the thirteenth century by the genius and humility of St Francis of Assisi, who will succeed in gathering up much of this popular aspiration and bringing it into the fold of the Church.

Meanwhile however, the dilemma remained. During the twelfth-century, Council after Council is held and condemns 'the errors of the heretics', and particularly those of Southern France who, from the Council of Tours in 1163 onwards, are known as 'Albigenses'. This name simply means the people of the ecclesiastical province of Albi, for it was natural to the Church to distinguish such movements according to their geographical distribution in the ecclesiastical provinces.

The position in Southern France was indeed at this time most serious from the point of view of the Church. Elsewhere the movements of revolt had as a rule the characteristics of popular revivalist outbursts and sooner or later burned out of themselves or succumbed before the hostility of the well-organized forces of Church and State. But in Southern France at this critical moment, when people were aspiring to a more ardent Christianity, not only did the Roman Church seem to have lost all sense of its mission, but a rival Church, claiming equal, or rather, superior Apostolic authority, was undertaking a systematic effort at conversion, and by the second half of the twelfth century had virtually displaced the Church of Rome as the recognized vehicle of the Christian revelation throughout Languedoc. This movement was Catharism, by far the most important of the anti-Catholic movements of the period. The Vaudois also played a large part in Southern France and at first they were included in the geographical term Albigensian. As time went on, however, this term came to be more and more applied as synonymous with Cathar. But the confusion and loose application of terms has tended to obscure the essential and significant difference between Catharism and contemporary revivalist movements, a difference which the Roman Church came to recognize as the greatest of all menaces to its authority. Though owing its rise and popularity to the general causes already mentioned, coupled with the social and political conditions prevailing in Languedoc at the time, Catharism was no spontaneous popular movement called into being by the haphazard inspiration of visionary enthusiasts or chance reformers; it was a definitely organized Church with a distinctive rite of admission and a trained priestly caste. It claimed to be nothing less than the true Church of Christ, its orders handed down in unbroken succession from the Apostles and retaining the power, which the false Church of Rome had lost or never possessed, of 'baptizing with the Holy Ghost and with fire'. Against this stupendous claim and the success of its ministers the Catholic Church found itself obliged to mobilize all its resources, finally raising against it a Crusade which was pursued more relentlessly than any against the Saracen infidel, and then creating an Inquisition to hunt down Cathars to the last man even in the trackless valleys and impenetrable caves of the Pyrenees, never resting till it was satisfied that the last of them had been exterminated.

But before considering this life and death struggle of two rival conceptions of Apostolic Christianity it is necessary to enter a word of caution. In all the records we possess of Councils and decrees condemning the heretics we find they are invariably denounced by listing the 'errors' in their beliefs. This reveals a fundamental misunderstanding which has never been properly appreciated. From the point of view of the doctors and bishops of the Catholic Church, imbued with theological training, doctrine assumes a predominant place, and when faced with criticism or opposition it is their natural reaction to refute it by exposing the intellectual 'errors' of the critics. The scholars who study these problems also bring to them a background of intellectual training. The result is that the doctrines professed by the heretics have been given, both then and now, a disproportionate importance. The ignorance and simplicity of the mass of the people at that time is overlooked. For the most part the common people were too ignorant and emotional to have a consistent theology or to attach much importance to it. For them it was life that mattered, not doctrine. They wanted intensely to live the Christian life, and if they could not live it in the Roman Church, then they would follow whoever provided an inspiring example. But, as we have seen, strange germs were in the air at this period, and in the fever of emotional revivalism many of them were caught. The church fastened on these as the weak joints in the heretics' armour and denounced them as 'damnable errors', while modern scholars have expended untold ingenuity in elaborating the theological systems of the Albigensian and other heresies.

In this way the ground of the debate has been shifted. Catholicism, then as now, has preferred to fight this duel on questions of dogma and belief, and because its cause has triumphed and only the Catholic record of the battle has survived, it is on these grounds that Catharism is still debated and judged. But this conception misses the whole point at issue. For Catharism, doctrine was secondary. What they stressed was life and example. For them the true disciples of Christ were those who copied His life and example, reverenced His teaching, and lived in strict obedience to it. The greatest of their bishops, Guilabert of Castres, when challenged, at the famous debate at Pamiers in 1207, to state his doctrine is said to have answered:

I have left father, mother and children, I have given up everything the Gospel commands me to renounce, gold and silver I no longer carry in my purse. I am satisfied with each day's food and am not anxious whether tomorrow I shall have the wherewithal to be clothed and fed. You behold in me the beatitudes which Jesus Christ preached and in which His Gospel consists. You see me poor, meek, peaceable, pure in heart, you see me in tears suffering hunger and thirst, persecution and the world's hatred for the sake of Righteousness.

This famous reply, apocryphal though it may perhaps be, very well sums up the essence of the Catharist creed. Christ redeemed mankind, not by His death but by His life, and man finds salvation not by expressing belief in a Son of God who suffered and died to atone for the sins of humanity, but by ordering his life according to the pattern set by a Divine Exemplar.

That this conception involved a theory of Redemption, a Christology and a cosmology radically different from the orthodox was essentially subordinate, and because it was subordinate we shall find considerable divergences of view and inconsistencies of thought when we come to examine it in detail. The Cathar view of the universe was not so watertight and logically consistent as the Catholic, and, while its simplicity appealed to the common man of the period, it was not the best weapon with which to oppose Catholicism. Since, however, the latter had choice of ground and weapons, the duel was perforce fought on this issue.

The Catharist metaphysical system, like the Catholic, had a long history of borrowing and development behind it; but whereas Catholic theology had placed Christ in a cosmic framework drawn from Judaeo-Hellenistic philosophy and its cult had undergone accretions from the Roman development of Solar Mithraism and the Graeco-Egyptian mysteries of Isis, the Catharist stream, starting from the same fountain-head, had flowed in a different direction and received its tributaries from Asian Gnosticism and Persian dualism, and was therefore less well adapted to the European mind. All this is dealt with more fully later. Here it is sufficient to remark that the Roman Church saw in Catharism a re-emergence of that Manichaeism against which it had already fought a deadly battle in the fourth and fifth centuries, a struggle which had played no small part in stimulating the development of Catholic theology.

But all this is quite irrelevant to an explanation of the success of Catharism against Catholicism in twelfth-century Languedoc. To explain that, all that is necessary is to compare the picture of practical Christianity presented by the two Churches to an age avid for a vital religion. For the Roman we cannot do better than quote Pope Innocent III himself, the Pope who called down the Crusade against the Albigenses, and who thus describes the Archbishop of Narbonne and the clergy of his province,

Simoniacs who sell justice, absolve the rich and condemn the poor. They do not keep even the laws of the Church. They accumulate benefices and entrust the priesthood and ecclesiastical dignities to unworthy priests and illiterate children. Hence the insolence of the heretics; hence the contempt of nobles and people for God and His Church. In this region prelates are the laughing stock of the laity . . . the Archbishop of Narbonne knows no other God than money, his heart is a bank.

In contrast to this was the life and character of the Cathars, whose name means 'Pure' from the Greek *Katharos*. This name was strictly applied only to those who had received the Consolamentum or Baptism of the Spirit. These alone formed the Church, and they acted as ministers of religion to the mass of the people who were simply

Credents or Believers. The true Cathari were usually called Perfecti by the Catholics, while to their own followers they were known simply as the 'Good Men' or the 'Good Christians'. Their aim above all was to live the pure life in strict obedience to the teachings of Christ. Renouncing all worldly possessions they devoted themselves not only to an active ministry of preaching, but to healing the sick, teaching the young, and aiding the people even in their manual labour, asking nothing in return. They travelled the country indefatigably, carrying no money, seeking no reward save the joy of winning souls for Christ, shirking no sacrifice and subjecting themselves to the most rigid asceticism.

It is hardly surprising therefore to find all authorities agreed that in the fifty years preceding the Albigensian Crusade practically the whole population of Languedoc had been won over to the Cathars or the Vaudois. Catholic churches were abandoned, sometimes falling into ruins and sometimes even used for heretical services, particularly by the Vaudois. Cathar and Vaudois ministers preached openly; their ceremonies were held publicly, and in many places the one or the other had in effect become the official religion. While they frequently operated alongside, and sometimes in rivalry, the Vaudois appear to have concentrated more on the region to the North of Toulouse and were particularly strong in Montauban and Moissac, while Catharism operated more particularly eastward and southward from Toulouse. While enjoying the support of a majority in the large towns like Toulouse, Albi, Béziers, and Carcassonne, the adherence of the population to Catharism was practically total in most of the smaller towns, notably: Lavaur, Avignonnet, Castelnaudary, Laurac, Fanjeaux, Mirepoix, Saissac, Cabardes, and Minerve. The Roman Church was incapable of reacting, for the higher clergy were related to the noble families who themselves favoured the Cathars, while the lower clergy, living in the midst of a population completely won over to the heresy, were helpless, discouraged, and apathetic.

The Papacy therefore found itself obliged to intervene and endeavoured to combat this state of affairs by condemnations pronounced in successive Councils and by the dispatch of preaching missions. As early as 1147 Pope Eugenius III, alarmed at the progress of the heresy in Southern France, appointed two legates, Alberic of Cluny and Geoffrey of Chartres, assisted by the celebrated St Bernard, to proceed on a preaching mission to the Midi. When the cardinal-legate Alberic preached in the Cathedral of Albi only thirty people attended, while St Bernard was booed in the streets of Toulouse and has left us this picture of the state of affairs from the Catholic point of view: 'The churches are without congregations, the people without priests, the priests without honour. There remain only Christians without Christ.

The sacraments are scorned, feasts no longer observed. Men die in their sins and children are deprived of life in Christ by refusing them the grace of baptism.' On the other hand, speaking of the Cathars, St Bernard says: 'Examine their mode of life, you will find nothing more irreproachable.'

This and other preaching missions proved completely ineffective so long as the Church persisted in putting doctrine before life. No amount of learned sermonizing or irrefutable theological reasoning could persuade people that a Church whose leaders lived luxurious lives and went about in fine clothes followed by imposing retinues of servants was more Christian than the 'good men' who had renounced the material world and who came before the people with nothing but their faith and their ardour.

In 1179 the third Lateran Council made the first appeal to the secular arm to aid the Church against 'the heretics whom some call Cathars, others Paterini and others Publicans,[1] who have made great progress in Gascony, the Albigeois, the country of Toulouse and elsewhere, where they publicly teach their errors and endeavour to pervert the simple. We declare them anathema, together with their protectors and abettors.' The Cardinal of Albano, appointed as legate, in addition to sending preachers all over Languedoc, gathered an armed force to attack the castle of Lavaur, a Cathar centre held by the Viscountess of Carcassonne. For the local lords, when not actually committed to Catharism themselves, were sympathetic to it and allowed the 'good men' to preach freely under their protection. This favour of the local nobility was due also in no small part to political and material considerations. The condemnation by Cathars and Vaudois of the wealth and property of the Church provided the rapacious barons who envied that property with a convenient justification for seizing it, and like the German princes who supported the Reformation in the sixteenth century, many of the Languedocian nobles of the twelfth century gave their approval and support to Catharism from similar mixed motives.

In 1198 Pope Innocent III was enthroned in St Peter's. To his outstanding ability, ruthless zeal, and tireless energy was added the most exalted conception of his sacred office. For him the Papacy was the divinely appointed and absolute master of Christendom, whose kings were but instruments for executing the will of God expressed through His Vicar on Earth. Innocent was determined that no effort must be spared to regain Southern France for the Church of Rome. From his accession the preaching missions became continuous and as the local hierarchy was ineffective (we have already seen Innocent's views on it) the powers of the Papal legates were gradually extended until they could depose bishops and excommunicate seigneurs who refused to act against the heretics, putting their lands under interdict. From this it was but a short step to enjoining the people to 'take arms against the heretics when the legates order it' and indulgences were accorded to those who should obey such a command. For over a hundred years the popes had preached the Crusade and granted indulgences to those who fought for Christ against the Moslem infidel. Was not the Manichaean heretic as great a menace to Christendom as the Saracen or the Moor? But when this final step was taken and a regular Crusade preached against Southern France we shall find that political considerations at once came into play and the Holy War was transformed into a secular struggle in which the barons of Northern France sought to expropriate the lords of the South, and the king of France to consolidate his kingdom by bringing Languedoc under his immediate rule. We must first therefore sketch the political background to the Albigensian Crusade.

In the twelfth century the greatest lord in what had been Gaul was not the King of France but the Count of Toulouse, whose domains extended from the Garonne to the Rhone, from the Pyrenees and the Mediterranean to the Lot and the Massif Central. All this he held as nominal vassal to the King of France just as the English kings held Aquitaine, Anjou, and Normandy by a similar anomalous tenure in which the vassal was more powerful than his nominal suzerain. In addition, as Marquis of Provence, which he held of the Holy Roman Emperor, the Count of Toulouse extended his sway to the borders of Italy. In those days this southern realm was more closed to the north than it is today by the vast, trackless, and dangerous forests which then covered Auvergne and the Massif Central, and the only convenient access to it from the region of Paris was by the Rhone valley. By contrast it was more open to communication with Spain and the Mediterranean, and the ports of Narbonne and Saint-Gilles, now silted up, pursued a flourishing trade with the Levant and all the lands of the inland sea. The population, in which the primitive Celtiberian was blended with strains of Roman, Arab, and Jew, was more mixed, more evolved, more refined, its horizons wider than that of the still crude and rustic north, and it can fairly be claimed that at this period Languedoc was in many respects the most civilized part of Western Europe. More than anywhere else, with the possible exception of Italy, it had conserved the imprint of Rome and been less affected by the anarchy of the Dark Ages. From the appalling raids of the Vikings and the Magyars it had happily been free, and although commerce and city life had foundered here as elsewhere in the first centuries of the Dark Ages, they were now reviving with alacrity, while in the north society still remained predominantly rural. Avignon, Nimes, Montpellier, Béziers, Narbonne, Carcassonne, and Toulouse were almost city-states on the Italian model, ruled by consuls selected from an already opulent commercial class which disputed the authority of the feudal lords. The gentry, becoming more cultured and courtly, were finding time for more refined pleasures than war and hunting, and it is this period and region which saw the rise of the amorous courtly poetry of the Troubadours, heralds of the dawn of European literature.

This advance in civilization of Southern France over the North was, however, temporary, and should not be too greatly exaggerated. The constant menace of Viking raids, if it had temporarily retarded the blooming of northern civilization, had welded the North more compactly into the feudal system and made it tougher and more homogeneous. This greater cohesion and centralization was to prove a powerful weapon in the hands of such capable monarchs as Philip II, Louis VIII, and Louis IX, who used it as the nucleus for building the modern realm of France and enjoyed by its means a decisive advantage over the loose and inchoate dominions of the Counts of Toulouse. The latter, though powerful in theory, were in fact weakened by the semi-independence of the great cities, by the chronic rebelliousness of their own vassals, and by the constant breaking down of large estates because of the complicated pattern of inheritance. In addition, the kings of Aragon in Spain, who already ruled the Roussillon and whose dominions therefore straddled the Pyrenees, were intriguing to extend their power, and we constantly find them in alliance with the principal vassals of Toulouse. In particular the House of Trencavel was a continual menace to the integrity of the Toulousain domain, for it held no less than four viscounties, Béziers, Carcassonne, Albi, and the Razés (the region stretching south-westwards from Carcassonne to the Pyrenees), which formed a solid block cutting the domains of Toulouse in two. When therefore the Catholic Church, finally exasperated by the progress of the Albigensian heresy, called the lords of Northern France to its aid in a holy war, these divisions proved fatal to a united defence and the seigneuries of the Midi fell piecemeal, to the ultimate profit of the centralizing policy of the French monarchy.

The story of the Cathar Church is therefore inseparably bound up with the history of French unity and with the struggle of the Romance civilization against the more robust and determined Frank. As a result, the Albigensian Crusade and the events leading up to it have been denatured by partisan accounts. While it has passed into the history of France as a mere episode in the story of French unity, in reaction against this view the local patriotism of the South has seen in it the heroic struggle of *la patrie romane* whose refined and superior civilization was submerged by brutal and barbarous hordes from the north avid to plunder and expropriate the wealth and lands of

Languedoc, and for whom the Crusade against the heretic was but a pretext. On the religious side, Catholics excuse it as the only means of delivering the helpless and ignorant people from the odious and diabolical corruption of the sectaries, the logical consequence of whose doctrines could only end in the extinction of human society, while on the other side the pure religion of the spirit is depicted as being ruthlessly exterminated in blood and fire, the inevitable atrocities of medieval warfare are magnified into stupendous and unexampled horrors, and every exaggeration of romance and pseudo-mysticism has been evoked by the 'Crusade against the Grail'.

But the Crusade was not launched until Innocent III had exhausted every possible means of winning over the people by persuasion. He chose as legates Cistercian monks who displayed the utmost zeal and courage and who finally adopted the novel method of challenging the Cathars to a number of public debates. The first of these was held at Carcassonne in 1204 in the presence of King Pedro II of Aragon and a great audience of the local nobility and bourgeois. The rival parties selected from the audience a jury composed of thirteen Catholics and an equal number of Catharist Credents, and the debate appears to have ranged with the utmost freedom over all the points of doctrine and practice which divided the two denominations. Unfortunately, both for this and for the similar debates which followed in the next three years, we have been left in ignorance of the exact nature of the arguments used, of the course of the debate, and of the decisions of the jury. Peter de Vaux-Cernay and Guy de Puylaurens, the Catholic chroniclers whose accounts alone survive, merely state that the heretics were refuted, a conclusion we may be permitted to doubt when instead of giving us details of the debate and the finding of the jury they prefer to describe the miracles which attested the truth of the Catholic arguments and accuse the umpires of partiality for the Cathars. At all events, it seems clear that this method was no more successful than the rest in winning the people back to the Catholic faith. Appealing though it is to the modern mind, it shows once again the ineradicable Roman conception that religion is a matter of doctrine and argument instead of one of life and conduct. In 1205 we find the disheartened and discouraged legates bewailing their lack of success to the Spanish Bishop of Osma who was at Montpellier on his return from a mission in Eastern Europe. He at once laid his finger on the weakness of the legates' case and of the Church of Rome: 'Go and teach,' he said, 'after the example of the Divine Master, in humility on foot, not with a sumptuous retinue, but penniless like the Apostles.'

The Abbot of Citeaux replied that if someone would give the lead, he would follow. The Bishop of Osma at once sent away his own retinue, and retaining only his sub-prior, the future St Dominic, declared himself ready to set the example of preaching in evangelistic simplicity and poverty in imitation of the Cathars. The Pope at once approved the new venture, indeed may have indirectly suggested it, and from it grew the Order of St Dominic or the Preaching Friars.[2] This order was founded with the specific object of combating the Albigensian heresy, first winning the people by copying its tactics and then instructing them in the Catholic faith. For St Dominic was impressed above all by the ignorance and simplicity of the people, and from his point of view this ignorance was the root-cause of the trouble.

In the next two years seven public debates were held in which Dominic and the Cistercian legates confronted the best champions of Catharism, notably Guilabert de Castres, Cathar bishop of Toulouse and the most prominent Catharist leader during the stormy period of the Crusade.[3]

The last and greatest debate was held at Pamiers in the castle of the Count of Foix, whose sister Esclarmonde, herself an initiated Cathar, took part on the Catharist side. She had received the Consolamentum at Fanjeaux in 1205 in a great ceremony attended by all the nobility of the region and she became the most powerful patroness of Catharism, founding with her sister-in-law, the Countess of Foix, a convent for Catharist women, and it was her Pyrenean castle of Montségur which, in the stormy years of the Crusade became the 'lighthouse' and last stronghold of the armed defenders of her faith. She has passed into legend as a sort of high priestess of Catharism and guardian of the Holy Grail.[4]

While the energy and zeal of Dominic, and his inspiration of fighting the Cathars on their own ground, proved a great deal more effective than the efforts of previous Catholic champions, and indeed effected a number of conversions, it was apparent that Catharism had secured too firm a hold on the country to be seriously shaken. The local rulers were too strongly on its side for the anathemas of the legates and threats of excommunication, when not backed by physical force, to induce them to take action against the great majority of their own subjects. But Innocent III was quite prepared, if all other methods failed, to use force in what he considered the sacred cause of Christendom which, to him, was identified with the Papal authority, and Raymond VI, the feeble, vacillating, and pleasure-loving Count of Toulouse, despite his sympathy for Catharism, proved amenable to a threat which Innocent had not hesitated to apply even to kings. The Papacy, in excommunicating a temporal ruler, could declare him deposed and his possessions forfeit to whoever seized them. Already on several occasions Innocent had called on the King of France to bring his vassal to order and compel him to obey the Church by expelling the heretics from his dominions. For the moment Philip II had his hands full with his struggle to consolidate the French monarchy against the double menace of England and the Empire. But the time came when he was free to turn his attention southwards, and nothing suited him better than an excuse to annex the wide domains of Toulouse and round off the rising centralized monarchy of France.

In January 1208 matters were brought to a head when Pierre de Castelnau, the Papal legate, after solemnly excommunicating the Count of Toulouse, was murdered by one of the latter's knights. The Pope at once called upon the King of France to drive the Count of Toulouse from his lands and give them to good Catholics. 'who under your happy rule will faithfully serve the Lord'. At the same time Arnaud-Amaury, the Abbot of Cîteaux, proclaimed the Crusade to the barons of the North. Philip II, in declining a personal participation in the Crusade on the grounds of his other preoccupations, was careful to remind the Pope that he must not presume to dispose of lands of which he (the king) was the suzerain without consulting him. Under this reserve he will allow his barons to respond to the Pope's appeal for a holy war against the Albigenses.

Faced with the menace of the assembling forces of a Crusade Raymond VI determined to make his peace and humbly sought reconciliation with the Church. After delivering seven castles as a hostage and undergoing a humiliating penance, his excommunication was lifted and he added his presence to the forces of the Crusade. This defection rendered impossible any hope of a united front against the northern invasion, and only the young Ramon-Roger Trencavel, Viscount of Béziers and Carcassonne, dared to oppose the first onslaught of the Crusade by force of arms. Raymond probably flattered himself that his policy was both prudent and advantageous, but in fact it was short-sighted as well as cowardly. Dilettante and epicurean himself, he was quite unable to appreciate the moral fervour of the Crusaders or the determination of the Papacy to exterminate Catharism. He perhaps imagined the Crusade would be over in one campaign, after which the Northerners would return home with their plunder, leaving him to consolidate a domain rendered more homogeneous by the elimination of his rival Trencavel, whose lands, as we have seen, formed an uncomfortable enclave in those of Toulouse. In the event, he merely played into the hands of his enemies by dividing the forces opposed to them, and eventually found himself obliged to face the Crusaders alone and unsupported.

In July 1209 the Army of the Cross assembled at Lyon under the command of Arnaud-Amaury, the Papal legate. The numbers are impossible to estimate, but even allowing for the fantastic exaggerations of chroniclers and partisan historians, they must have been considerable for the period. A Crusade was always a popular venture, for with participation went automatically a plenary indulgence, and in this case the attraction of securing such a reward was offered without the perils of a journey to the East. But it must be remembered that the overwhelming majority of the army were supernumeraries, adventurers, and camp followers, who joined the host in the hope of winning plunder or salvation, and who cannot be counted as effective fighting troops. These were made up of the feudal levies, the barons and knights and their immediate retainers, who numerically were but a fraction of the total and who, for the most part, regarded their service as accomplished when they had completed the forty days prescribed by feudal usage.

The army descended the Rhone and entered Montpellier, which was still largely a Catholic city, without opposition. On 22 July the Crusaders arrived before Béziers, which closed its gates. But the over-confidence of the citizens led them to attempt a sortie which, being repulsed, they were driven back in disorder and the Crusaders entered the city and captured it in the ensuing panic. A general massacre followed, and the Papal legate, in answer to the query how Catholics were to be distinguished from heretics, is said to have made the famous reply, 'Kill them all, God will know His own.'

The rapid and dramatic fall of the important city of Béziers spread alarm throughout Languedoc, and the city of Narbonne, together with the lords of nearly one hundred castles, hastened to make their submission to the legate.

The Crusaders immediately marched on Carcassonne where the young Viscount Trencavel had concentrated his forces and trusted to the formidable fortifications of the city to defy any siege. But a large number of non-combatants had crowded in from the neighbouring countryside, and once the besiegers had cut off the outside water supply the besieged were reduced to rain-supplied tanks. In the August heat and drought dysentery broke out in the overcrowded city and within a fortnight the gallant Viscount was obliged to sue for terms.

After the fall of Carcassonne some smaller towns such as Limoux, Montréal, and Castres surrendered without a fight. But if the viscounties of Béziers and Carcassonne were thus subdued, a number of castles in the Black Mountains to the north and in the foothills of the Pyrenees to the south defied the Crusade and offered the protection of their walls to the Cathars who hastened to take refuge in them. Meanwhile the bulk of the crusading army, its forty days of feudal service accomplished, was returning to the north. Simon de Montfort, a baron of the Ile de France and titular Earl of Leicester, who had been installed as Viscount of Carcassonne and Béziers in place of the hapless Trencavel, who died still a captive in unexplained circumstances, found himself entering upon an uneasy possession. His only permanent forces in the midst of a hostile population were the barons and knights to whom the confiscated castles and fiefs of Trencavel's vassals had been assigned and who were therefore dispersed in numerous small garrisons. Although the Church continued to preach the Crusade and each summer would bring a reinforcement of knights from the north, zealous to strike a blow for Christ and obtain the promised indulgence, these melted away after performing their forty days service, and for the rest of the year de Montfort had to rely almost entirely on mercenaries. He enjoyed, however, the moral and material support of the Church, which never failed to provide him with funds and diplomatic backing. But his strongest arm was his own tireless energy and ability. He was a born leader, animated by a burning zeal for the cause he served, while against him the nobles of the south were divided and vacillating, each seeking only his own personal safety and advantage.

Had they been able to combine, and had Raymond VI been capable of a little energy, courage, and leadership, Montfort's position would have been quite untenable. But *le patriotisme roman* was as yet inexistent, or at least inchoate, and was in fact largely called into being in reaction against the French conquest which the Crusade in effect became. Even so, after the departure of the bulk of the Crusading forces, Montfort was reduced for the winter to a precarious defensive. The barons of the south were incensed at what they considered the murder of Trencavel and alarmed for their own possessions, while they were secretly encouraged by the King of Aragon who hoped to extend his own sway over Languedoc, or at least prevent it from falling under the direct influence of the French crown. Several weakly held castles were recaptured, but Montfort restored the situation with the help of reinforcements which reached him in the following summer, and doggedly, systematically consolidated the conquest of the four Trencavel viscounties, which was complete by the end of 1211.

Montfort then turned his attention to Toulouse, which had always been considered the nerve-centre of the heretical movement. Raymond VI had saved himself in 1209 by his abject submission, but since then he had failed to keep the promises he had made to repress the heresy in his dominions. While he hesitated and temporized, vainly seeking some way of deflecting the menace which hung over him, Montfort secured a number of his castles and, with his numbers swollen by the arrival of the summer contingent, marched on Toulouse. But if the Count was weak, the citizens under the leadership of their consuls were more resolute and determined to defend the city. Aided by the Count of Foix they successfully defied the Crusade and Montfort was obliged to raise the siege. Infuriated, he marched against Foix, burned the town, and devastated the countryside, though leaving the castle of Foix unattacked. He then occupied Cahors and the Quercy.

Meanwhile, pushed by the rising anti-French sentiment of the people, the Count of Toulouse assembled his vassals and all the dispossessed and threatened barons of Languedoc into an army which should have had a decisive numerical superiority over the depleted and scattered forces of Montfort. But in a pitched battle at Castelnaudary Montfort triumphed once more. In 1212 he subdued the Agenais and Comminges while Raymond, lacking the energy and the resources to prevent his progress, found himself more and more hemmed in. Holding only Toulouse and Montauban, cut off from Provence, unable to pay his mercenaries, and with the majority of his vassals reduced to the status of guerrillas, his situation was indeed desperate. In these circumstances he crossed the Pyrenees and appealed for help to Pedro II, King of Aragon. This king, who had just won a crushing victory over the Moors and greatly extended his dominions in Spain, could not view with a favourable eye the installation of the barons of Northern France in the Languedoc, over which he already enjoyed a considerable influence and hoped to extend his authority. After using his influence at the Roman court to rouse the Pope against the excesses of the Crusaders he crossed the Pyrenees with a powerful army.

This intervention on the heretic side of a Catholic monarch in high favour at Rome shows that the Albigensian Crusade had already become more of a political than a religious struggle; and when in September 1213 Pedro II was defeated and slain at Muret by the ever-victorious Montfort his defeat was of international importance, for it decided that after the death of Montfort it should be the French kings and not the Spanish who would be heirs to the lands of the Midi.

After the battle of Muret the Counts of Foix and Comminges and the Count and Consuls of Toulouse submitted and took an oath before the Papal legate and the Archbishop of Narbonne to pursue the heretics in their cities, while Montfort subdued the Rouergue and completed the conquest of the whole of Languedoc. But the Pope was not anxious to see Montfort become sole monarch of the whole country and would not permit him to substitute himself for the Count of Toulouse, while the legates took good care that it should be the Church which received the submission and took possession of the personal castles of the Counts of Foix and Toulouse. But now the King of France, delivered by his victories at Bouvines and La Roche-aux-Moines from the double menace of the German Emperor and the English king, felt at liberty to turn his attention to these southern regions of his nominal domain, now subdued by the efforts of his own more immediate vassals. The time was ripe to show his flag in the South, to consolidate the conquest in the centralizing interests of the Crown, and make effective a suzerainty so long merely nominal.

In 1215 Prince Louis, the future Louis VIII, took the Cross and made his pilgimage to the South at the head of a considerable army. The fighting was now over for the time being and this Crusade was nothing but a triumphal progress. But politically it was decisive and perfectly timed. It was a warning to the Pope that Languedoc was not to be considered a fief of the Church and a reminder to the northern barons, who might be toying with the hope of simply replacing the southern lords in their semi-independent seigneuries, that the King of France was their overlord. To the people the authority of the Crown was welcome as promising a check upon the harsh repacity of their new northern lords and the intolerance of the Roman legates. In 1216 Simon de Montfort, determined that he and not the Church should rule in the lands he had subdued, went to Paris and there solemnly did homage to Philip II for all the lands of the Count of Toulouse and was confirmed in the titles of the latter as direct vassal of the king.

But Raymond VI having settled his claims on his son, the young Raymond VII was acclaimed with enthusiasm by the cities of Provence, which flared into revolt. Before the city of Beaucaire on the Rhone Simon de Montfort in person was repulsed after a lengthy and fruitless siege, and at the news Toulouse revolted and declared for Raymond VII. The Crusade was now officially considered to be over and the war therefore assumes a purely patriotic and dynastic aspect. Montfort has become merely a territorial lord coping with domestic insurrection and can no longer count on the armed support of distant Crusaders but must rely on his own resources.

These proved completely inadequate against the awakened patriotism of the South, which rapidly took the character of a general popular revolt. And when Simon de Montfort fell in 1218 before the defiant walls of Toulouse the odds proved too great for his son Amaury, who was utterly incapable of standing before the storm. The feeble and scattered garrisons of his castles were swept away one after another, often by local patriotic uprisings, and within a few years Raymond VII, his forces increasing with each success, had recovered all the lands of his father. Even a royal army under Prince Louis, hastening to the assistance of the new and hard-pressed vassal of the Crown, was repulsed before Toulouse and obliged to raise the siege. By 1224 Amaury de Montfort was obliged to negotiate the surrender of Carcassonne, his last fortress, which was restored to the heir of Trencavel, and betook himself with a handful of surviving northern knights to the court of France where he readily ceded all his rights to

King Louis VIII in exchange for a pension and an office.

The King of France had thus acquired in due legal form the rights to direct rule in Languedoc. It remained to conquer the land. The Papacy was by no means anxious to see the French monarchy extend its power so far and was quite prepared for a reconciliation with Raymond VII, who had never shown any hostility to the Roman Church, if he would for his part repress the heresy in his dominions. But although, unlike his father, he seems never to have had any personal inclination towards Catharism as a religion, it was undeniable that the heresy had received a notable encouragement from the success of his arms, and the influence of the episcopacy of Languedoc was therefore exerted against him at the Vatican. In a Council at Bourges in 1226 the Papal legate and the assembled bishops solemnly confirmed the Lateran decree of 1215 declaring Raymond excommunicated and deposed and, Amaury de Montfort having ceded his claims, the King of France was invited to take possession of the land and accorded all the spiritual support given to a Crusade.

The way thus prepared, Louis VIII set out once more for the South at the head of a powerful army. At his approach cities and barons hastened to make their submission and Raymond was rapidly abandoned by the greater part of his subjects. But the sudden death of the king saved Toulouse and Raymond was able to conserve his capital and his title. Nevertheless, the whole of Northern and Eastern Languedoc, including all the domains of Trencavel, was by this expedition firmly united to the Crown. Raymond was, however, far from acknowledging defeat, and as soon as the bulk of the royal army had withdrawn he took the offensive, aided by the Count of Foix. But the odds were now too unequal and three years later Raymond submitted and made his peace with the Church and the king. By the Treaty of Meaux (1229) he conserved only the city and neighbourhood of Toulouse, which at his death was to pass with his daughter to the king's brother and ultimately to the Crown.

What, meanwhile, had become of the Cathars? Before 1209 we have seen Catharism functioning openly as an established Church enjoying respect and support in every class of society, its ceremonies attended by large congregations and its leaders invited by the Papal legates to defend their faith in public debates. But with the arrival of the crusade all this was changed. A Crusade is of necessity a fanatical enterprise and men who have been persuaded to take the cross to fight the enemies of God do so consumed with righteous anger and are out for blood. The orders of the Pope to his legate Arnaud-Amaury were to 'drive out' the heretics, which may explain the bloodless surrender negotiated at Carcassonne. But this could afford no satisfaction to the Crusaders, nor was it, from the point of view of the Church, any real solution, since it merely dispersed the heretics instead of extirpating them. On the other hand further indiscriminate massacres like that of Béziers could clearly not be countenanced either.

The solution which reconciled these difficulties was that adopted when the castle of Minerve was captured in 1210. The conditions of capitulation were that the fighting men should go free and Catharist Credents would also be free on condition they made their submission to the Church. As for the true Cathars, 'clothed heretics', as they were called on account of their distinctive dress, they were to have the choice of abjuration or being burned at the stake. The Abbot of Vaux-Cernai made an effort to preach to the latter in an attempt to save them, but they refused to listen to him and hurled themselves voluntarily into the fire. At Minerve those who thus perished were more than one hundred and forty, both men and women.

Thereafter this became the usual procedure and the capture of each castle was accompanied by the burning 'with great joy' according to the chronicler, of the Cathars who had taken refuge in it. There was no trial, neither did the Cathars seek to dissemble their quality or hesitate to affirm their faith, and invariably went into the fire of their own accord without even requiring to be led to it. The greatest holocaust was at Lavaur in 1211 where between three and four hundred perished at the stake while the Catharist chatelaine was thrown into a well and stoned to death.

In this manner the élite of the Cathar Church was destroyed in the course of the Crusade. The Catholic historian Belperron estimates as at least one thousand the number of the 'Pure' who thus perished summarily with the capitulation of the strongholds in which they had sought refuge. But many still remained in fortresses as yet unsubdued, and particularly at Montségur and in the Corbières. From these secure refuges they made excursions whenever possible to encourage their adherents, but now they were obliged to act secretly and move with caution. The distinctive dress was abandoned and replaced by the *kosti*, a symbolical girdle worn under the clothes. As soon, however, as Raymond VII had reconquered a large part of his dominions they resumed their open activity and even reopened their convent communities at Fanjeaux, Laurac, and Castelnaudary. Guilabert of Castres, Bishop of Toulouse and head of the Catharist Church in Languedoc, with his *filius major* (i.e. designated successor) Bertrand En Marti, were most in evidence at this time. In the reaction against the conquest, Catholic became in great measure synonymous with French and Romance patriotism was therefore favourable to Catharism, the resurgence of which in its turn favoured the patriotic liberation.

But the Treaty of Meaux was for Catharism a mortal blow. Raymond VII was obliged by its terms to take a solemn engage-ment to pursue the heretics in his dominions. Moreover, up till then the civil powers had merely been expected to take action against open and notorious heretics. Now a new principle is introduced. It is an obligation of every good Catholic to reveal any heretic he knows. The officials of the King and the Count of Toulouse are to seek them out and a substantial reward is offered for anyone who reveals a heretic and procures his condemnation. The Count of Foix, as a condition of peace, was obliged to accept the same terms, and a Council was convoked at Toulouse by the Papal legate which formulated forty-five canons for the purging of the country of heresy. These canons codified a whole procedure of search, pursuit, and repression, the first outlines of what shortly afterwards became the Inquisition.

The bishops were to appoint a priest and two laymen in each parish who were to take an oath to seek out heretics and their abettors, and for this purpose they were authorized to search houses, barns, cellars, anywhere they had reason to suspect a Cathar might be hiding. Those who gave shelter to a heretic were to have their houses burned and their goods confiscated. Any official who was not considered zealous enough in hunting out heretics was liable to the confiscation of his goods, while any lord on whose territory too many heretics were found was liable to lose his lands. Every man over fourteen and every woman over twelve was to take an oath of fidelity to orthodoxy and swear to seek out and denounce heretics. Those who failed to take this oath or who did not come to communion and confession three times a year were to be treated as suspected of heresy. No layman was to possess a copy of the Scriptures except a psalter, breviary, and the canonical Hours, and all in Latin. Catharists who were converted voluntarily to Catholicism were obliged to wear a yellow cross sewn on their clothes front and back, to live in a Catholic city, and to lose all civil rights. Those who were converted only after proceedings against them had been taken suffered imprisonment and the confiscation of their goods. Finally, no heretic was to practise as a doctor and persons dangerously ill were to be watched to prevent the approach of anyone who might confer the Consolamentum, and the making of wills was to be witnessed by a priest.

The collaboration of the civil and religious authority was thus organized for searching out and punishing heresy. At first this repression acted intermittently under the ordinary authority of the bishops. But in 1233 Gregory IX made it a permanent and continuous institution and entrusted its exercise to the Dominican Order acting in the name and authority of the Holy See.

But opposition still smouldered. The conquest and expropriation of the Languedocian nobles had created a class of dispossessed ex-seigneurs known as *faidits* whose one hope of recovering their lands lay in a successful revolt which the Cathars and their sympathisers, oppressed and tracked down by the Inquisition, were ever ready to support. Moreover, the rigour of the Inquisition everywhere roused the anger of the population, even Catholic, who did all they could to aid and conceal the 'good men' who seemed to symbolize and incarnate the popular hatred of French domination. So widespread was the connivance of the population that in 1234 further edicts were added to those of the Council of Toulouse, prescribing that every person in the locality where a heretic was captured should pay a silver mark to the person who indicated him, and any house where a Cathar was found alive or dead should be demolished and the goods of its owner confiscated.

The headquarters of the *faidits* and the Cathars was the castle of Montségur, built by Esclarmonde of Foix, and now commanded by Pierre-Roger de Mirepoix and Ramon de Perelha. Here Guilabert de Castres took up his residence in 1232 and reorganized the Cathar Church. The powerful fortress of Montségur, secure on its rocky peak 4000 feet high in the Pyrenees, became the last bastion at once of Romance patriotism and the Cathar Church.

Meanwhile in the towns the opposition to the Inquisition and the movement of resistance to the French occupation steadily gathered strength and culminated in 1235 in acts of violence. The consuls and people of Toulouse expelled the Dominicans and the bishop by force, while the Dominican convent at Narbonne was sacked by the people and similar outbreaks occurred at Albi and other cities. On several occasions arrested heretics were delivered from the Inquisition by popular uprisings, often with the complicity of the local authorities. Raymond VII, though he had been obliged to make a show of zeal in pursuing the Cathars, kept a close eye on the mounting popular anger and carefully prepared to exploit it for the recovery of his domains when it should be ripe for general revolt. Revolt broke out, however, independently of Raymond, in the former dominions of Trencavel. The royal officials who governed these lands were both ill paid and uncontrolled. Taxes were farmed out and the population exploited. Moreover, whenever a heretic was condemned to death it was the civil authorities who received his confiscated property, and this meant that the royal officials not only showed a zeal surpassing even that of the Inquisition in hunting down heretics, but even burned people who had been awarded lesser sentences by the Holy Office. Finally the southern cities had been accustomed to a municipal independence unknown in the north and the officials trained in administering the royal demesne showed scant respect for the privileges of the consuls and municipal authorities.

The young Viscount Trencavel, dispossessed heir to Carcassonne,

Albi, and Béziers, became the natural leader and rallying point of all the dispossessed lords who dreamed of returning to their family estates. When he appeared in Languedoc in the summer of 1240 they at once joined him. But after five unsuccessful assaults on Carcassonne he was obliged by the arrival of a royal army to raise the siege and return to Spain. Raymond VII had hesitated to commit himself, perhaps judging the moment premature as his own diplomatic preparations were not complete, and he took no action until 1242. Then, however, his secret alliances proved to have a foundation of sand, and the Count of Foix hastily made his peace with the king, transferring the county to the direct vassalage of the Crown. Raymond was obliged once more to make a humiliating submission.

Meanwhile, the *faidits* of Montségur, profiting by the revolt of Raymond, had made a sortie and massacred the Inquisitor of Toulouse with all his suite. After the submission of Raymond, therefore, the seneschal of Carcassonne resolved to destroy Montségur and after a heroic defence lasting over a year the castle was at last obliged to surrender on 2 March 1244. Two hundred and five Cathars, the last compact remnant of the Church of the Pure in Southern France, were burned including the Bishop Bertrand En Marti, who had succeeded Guilabert de Castres. His successor Victor took refuge in the obscure fortress of Quéribus in the Corbières, and when it too fell in 1255 the seat of the bishopric of Toulouse was removed to Italy.

After the abortive revolts of 1240 and 1242 and the fall of Montségur, the Inquisition in Languedoc was reinforced and the collaboration of the royal officials intensified. At the same time the last of the noble families who still offered their protection to the Cathars were vanquished and the situation of the latter became less and less tenable. At first they sought refuge in the nearer valleys of Aragon, but the Inquisition soon began to function there too. Moreover, episcopal and royal authority was strong in Spain and Catharism could never secure there the foothold it once had in Southern France.

In Italy, however, the situation was more favourable. Catharism had come to Languedoc in the eleventh century through Italy from the Balkans, and it had remained influential in Italy ever since. In fact all the sects we have seen arising in France had their counterparts in Italy, where the Cathars were known as Paterini. The growing importance of the towns and their political hostility to the Church were factors favourable to them, and we invariably find them on the Ghibeline side in the great secular struggle between Pope and Emperor which tore every Italian city into rival factions in the twelfth and thirteenth centuries. In all the cities allied to the Emperors Otto IV and Frederick II against the Papacy we find the Paterini flourishing. But while the movement was influential it never secured anything like the general popular hold it had obtained in Southern France, nor required such drastic measures to extirpate. The reasons for this were that the clergy, unlike those of twelfth-century Languedoc, were not slack and prepared to compromise with the heresy but were always active against it, while on the other hand in Italy there was more indifference to religion amounting quite often to complete atheism. There was not the same ardent faith seeking expression and anticlericalism was political rather than religious. In the course of their political struggles with the Papacy and ecclesiastical authorities so many towns had so often been put under interdict and subjected to ecclesiastical penalties that these things had ceased to have any meaning and merely added to the general indifference. The Paterini therefore might be favoured by the podestas and the wealthy governing classes of the anti-Papal cities on account of their political hostility to the Church, but this was a very different basis from that on which the strength of Catharism had been built in Southern France. In Italy they were often merely the allies or protégés of the local tyrants, while on the other hand the common people who formed the popular parties hostile to the tyrants were usually Catholic. The difference stands out at once when we compare the success of St Dominic and his Preaching Friars in Italy with his relative failure in Languedoc. There, after ten years preaching, he had only succeeded in gathering round him a dozen preachers without noticeably diminishing the prestige of the Cathars and Vaudois, and his Order owed its triumph to the swords of the Crusaders. But in Italy the Dominican Order enjoyed at once an outstanding success. We read that 'they went from town to town usually in pairs, assembled the people and preached to them anywhere, in the churches, the streets, the market places. Their fervour, their words, the holiness of their lives, their poverty and humility won all hearts.' We might be reading of the Cathars of Languedoc, but it was the Dominicans, who had learned from and copied the Cathar methods in France who, together with the Franciscans, successfully applied these methods in Italy and won for Catholicism that place in the hearts of the common people which the co-religionaries of Catharism had here failed to secure.

But French Cathars and Italian Paterini were the same Church and they remained constantly in communion. During the siege of Montségur the Paterini Bishop of Cremona sent a messenger of sympathy to the besieged, and after the fall of the castle many of the surviving Cathars of Languedoc fled to the comparative security of Lombardy. Commercial relations between the two countries were close and a number of nuncii, usually merchants, assured a regular liaison between the two branches of the Church. They provided guides and money for those who decided to emigrate, assured their reception, kept relatives in touch. We hear of one Raymond Maurel who thus acted as nuncius between Languedoc and Lombardy for more than a quarter of a century. Families desirous of emigrating would realize their capital and transfer it bit by bit to Italy by means of these nuncii. Many went to stay, but many also made the journey simply to receive the Consolamentum and return home, while we hear of one wealthy merchant who sent to Lombardy for a Cathar to come to him to confer the Consolamentum.

But if Catharism in Italy owed its relative security to political conditions it declined swiftly when these conditions changed. After the death of Frederick II in 1250 the Ghibeline party steadily lost influence while that of the Guelfs and the Pope increased. The Inquisition had already been organized and wherever the popular party in the cities triumphed over the local tyrant persecution and the burning of heretics would follow. The Pope now felt strong enough, for example, to take action against the notorious Ezzelino, tyrant of Milan. A Crusade was launched against him and after his defeat and death in 1258 the Cathar bishop of Vicenza and thirty Perfecti were burned, while others, including the Bishop of the Marchese, recanted. It is noticeable that the Italian Cathars were much more ready to recant and abjure their faith under the threat of persecution than had been those of Languedoc. Some of them even became Inquisitors themselves and devoted the rest of their lives to the extermination of the faith in which they had once been revered as Pure Christians. The most notable of these were Moneta of Cremona and Rainiero Sacchoni (who had been a bishop), both of whom placed their inside knowledge of the organization and doctrine of the Cathar Church at the disposal of its enemies. Altogether there was much less sincerity and more hypocrisy in thirteenth-century Italy, and we hear of people who were reputed for their orthodoxy and sanctity being discovered after their deaths to have been heretics. One such was only discovered in the course of official proceedings with a view to his canonization as a Saint!

Meanwhile the victory of Charles of Anjou, brother of Louis IX of France, in Sicily in 1268 meant that the full rigour of the Inquisition was applied in Southern Italy, while in 1274 the Papacy succeeded in placing a candidate of its own on the Imperial throne in the person of Rudolf of Hapsburg. With the support of Angevin and Hapsburg the Pope was at last master of Italy and the fall of Catharism was not long delayed.

The greatest centre of Lombard Catharism was on the shores of Lake Garda and particularly the peninsula of Sermione. Here Bernard Oliva, the exiled Bishop of Toulouse, had taken up his residence and it was also the seat of an Italian Catharist bishop and enjoyed the protection of the local lords. The Inquisitor of Verona sent a female spy to Sermione and she took the Consolamentum in order to discover all the secrets of the Church. The della Scala family of Verona then organized a military expedition which destroyed the centre and one hundred and seventy-four captured Cathars were burned in the arena at Verona on 13 February 1278. With the destruction of the Church at Sermione and that in the Valtelline valley near Como in the same year Italian Catharism was virtually extirpated, for its adherents were not of the same fibre as those of Southern France, who continued to nurse their faith despite all the rigours of the Inquisition for a hundred years after the defeat of their last political supporters. In the year 1300 the Pope Boniface VIII held a great Jubilee to celebrate the triumph of the Church over the powers which had threatened it and to affirm the supremacy of the Papacy over the whole of Christendom.

8

Faith and Doctrine

IN considering the doctrine and system of the Cathars we must bear in mind that practically the whole of the evidence on which any reconstruction of it must be based is derived from the Church which exterminated it as a dangerous rival: 'Of the two voices upon which the historian could count for information one has been entirely silenced. Only the other remains, and its impartiality is doubtful since it is the voice of judges too often become executioners.'[1]

The principal sources are the registers of the Inquisition. Most of these have been lost, but there survive in particular a document (No. 609) in the municipal library of Toulouse which covers the period 1242–7 in that district, and the registers of the Inquisition of Carcassonne preserved in the *Collection Doat* (MSS 25–8) at the Bibliothèque Nationale in Paris, which cover most particularly the periods 1273–4 and 1285–90. In addition there is the *Manual of the Inquisitor* written by Bernard Gui who was an Inquisitor in Toulouse and in Italy from 1306 to 1323 and who wrote his manual as a guide for other inquisitors in the handling of heretics. We have also a booklet known as the *Sum of Authorities* specially drawn up for the Franciscan and Dominican preachers who combated the heretics. This gave a detailed refutation of the main Cathar doctrines with New Testament texts in support. It is surely, however, a little naïve to say with Guiraud, 'We have only to take the negation of the propositions listed to form a good idea of Catharism.' Finally, Rainerio Sacchoni and Moneta of Cremona, both Cathar initiates who became Dominicans, wrote treatises. Although apostates and Italians, it is impossible to deny that they wrote with inside knowledge.

With regard to the Inquisition registers it is important to bear in mind that they are of comparatively late date. They represent Catharism when it was undergoing the corruption and degeneration inseparable from persecution. We must remember that the élite of the church had already perished during the Crusade, and the interrogations which survive are chiefly of those 'suspected' of heresy; that is, possible Credents. They were ignorant for the most part, easily trapped by leading questions, holding many half-understood views, confused and inconsistent under skilled cross-examination, and scared. Bernard Delicios, the great Franciscan critic of the Inquisition, said: 'The Apostles Peter and Paul, if brought before the Inquisition, would scarcely be able to justify themselves. It is no longer a matter of justice when interrogation has become the subtle art of setting traps into which guilty and innocent stumble alike.' Even Guiraud admits the possibility that peasants then as now were terrified when in a law-court:

Did not Inquisitors conduct enquiries with preconceived ideas and desiring them to end with conclusions known in advance for the sake of their cause? Did they not extort calumniating statements from accused and witnesses? Did the latter have the energy to brave torture and the stake and keep their statements to the strict truth in spite of everything? Is it not more likely that to get free of these terrible judges who questioned them, they answered them as they wanted to be answered and charged the heretics with crimes as odious as imaginary? Was this not moreover the surest means for them of earning a precious certificate of orthodoxy which would ensure their security for the future?

In spite of these considerations it is possible to make a reasonably accurate reconstruction of Cathar doctrines. It is noteworthy that the great mass of the Catholic documentation representing so many differences of time, place, and point of view all substantially concurs. The Inquisition register in the library of Toulouse shows that a complete inventory was made even in the tiniest hamlet of the beliefs, doctrines, organization, and activity of the Cathars over the preceding fifty years. One Inquisitor alone examined no fewer than 5638 sworn witnesses. As the main object of this enquiry was to obtain information the Inquisitors had no interest in obtaining false answers. Nor had the Church any interest in charging the heretics with beliefs they did not hold.

Let us admit that the Inquisitors and the Catholic historians are fair and scientific according to their lights and that they have presented us with an accurate picture, from their angle, of Cathar beliefs and doctrines. What sort of a picture should we have of Catholic Christianity if it had been exterminated by a rival religion convinced that its doctrines were a diabolical menace to the whole established order? Moreover, it must never be forgotten that this very emphasis on doctrine arises only because Catholicism triumphed. The Catholic Church always admitted that the conduct and morals of the Cathars were exemplary. Therefore, as they could not be attacked on these grounds, the attack was concentrated on doctrinal extravagances. But the whole point of Catharism was their conception that Christianity is a life lived, not a doctrine believed in. For them the life of Jesus was a model the good Christian must strive to copy, not a cosmic mystery which he must blindly accept on trust.

While not neglecting the evidence provided by these Catholic sources it is clear that the only really valid evidence can come from sources peculiar to Catharism. Of these we have two. The first and more important is the ritual of the Consolamentum, written in the Languedocian language, and published by Clédat in 1887, now in the library at Lyon (see Nelli, *Ecritures Cathares*, for a French translation). Nothing could be more orthodox. It is replete with quotations of the canonical scriptures and breathes the very atmosphere of primitive Christianity. The other is a Latin work, known as the 'Book of John'. While it is dualist in doctrine, a great deal of it is the New Testament *verbatim* and its dualism is a logical development of that already inherent in John and Paul.

In the eyes of Catholic theologians the most serious 'error' in Catharist beliefs was dualism, the belief in two gods, one good and perfect, creator of the spirit, the other evil or imperfect, creator of the material universe. This is a view which has made its appeal to Christians of all ages. The material universe is manifestly imperfect; how then can it be the creation of a Being who is both perfect and all-powerful? 'For why is all around us here/As if some lesser god had made the world/But had not force to shape it as he would.'

It was from this premiss that the problem was resolved by that stream of Christian tradition of which Catharism is the latest expression. Nothing that is not perfect can have been created by God. All that is evil or imperfect must therefore be the work either of a rebellious subordinate deity or of an eternal evil power in opposition to God, and this inferior creation must include the material universe and our physical bodies. But there were innumerable variations on this central idea, ranging from the absolute dualism of the Manichaeans, derived from Mazdeism with its opposition of two equally eternal powers of good and evil, through every variety of subordination to the Most High God postulated in the Creator. We have no need to examine all these varieties here. What is important to notice is that the very fact that so many varieties of belief have been signalized in the Inquisition records and other sources emphasizes that for the Cathars, unlike the Catholics, there was no rigid dogma in the domain of metaphysics. There was never any question for them of imposing belief in these ideas as obligatory on their Credents. They were rather free speculations, offered as a reasonable solution to the mystery of evil for those who wanted answers to metaphysical problems, but by no means as an article of faith. Guiraud, the Catholic historian of Catharism, admits that only the Cathar leaders could distinguish the different schools of thought within their own communion, and he adds: 'They preferred to insist on the practice which united them rather than the theologies which divided.'

When, therefore, we sketch a general outline of the Catharist metaphysical system it must be remembered that while the same basic idea underlies all their conceptions of the universe many variations in detail were current and equally accepted. We will, however, place our main reliance on the 'Book of John' so far as it takes us, for this is the only Catharist source dealing with their metaphysical ideas which remains to us.

This book purports to be a private revelation given by Jesus Christ to the 'beloved disciple' in answer to the questions he asked as he lay on the Lord's breast at the last supper. In it Christ describes how Satan, who was a glorious angel, desired to set himself up as equal to God. For this purpose he took the elements of earth, air, fire, and water, and with them created the material universe. Then he seduced a number of angels to leave Heaven and share his domain with him promising them, 'If ye will hearken unto me I will set my seat in the clouds and be like the Most High . . . and I will reign with you world without end.' Then, having created the earth and the animals as described in Genesis, 'he devised furthermore and made man in his likeness, and commanded an angel of the third heaven to enter into the body of clay. And he took thereof and made another body in the form of a woman, and commanded an angel of the second heaven to enter into the body of the woman. But the angels lamented when they beheld a mortal shape upon them and that they were unlike in shape. And he commanded them to do the deed of the flesh in the bodies of clay, and they knew not how to commit sin.' So Satan led them into Paradise and tempted them. In this manner it has come about that 'certain of the angels which fell do enter unto the bodies of women, and receive flesh from the lust of the flesh, and so is a spirit born of spirit, and flesh of flesh, and so is the kingdom of Satan accomplished in this world' and that 'holy ones were found having bodies of clay because of their transgression and therefore were delivered to death'.

Such in outline is one of the beliefs current among the Cathars as to the origin of sin and the material universe. [Satan 'drew with his tail the third part of the stars of heaven and did cast them to the earth' (Revelation 12:4).] There were, however, a number of alternative versions of the temptation which caused the angels to fall. The most usual was that Satan persuaded the angels to follow him to his new domain by showing them a woman and thus awakening carnal desires. But all were agreed that it was only the souls of the angels which fell and were imprisoned in the bodies of clay. Their spirits, being one with the divine nature, could not fall, but remained in Heaven. Man therefore is composed of three parts: a spirit which is divine and remains always in heaven, a soul which has been separated from its holy spirit by its evil will in following Satan, and a body which is merely the work of Satan and to be rejected. They emphatically denied the resurrection of the flesh which is mere corruption; 'Flesh and Blood cannot inherit the kingdom of Heaven' (1 Cor. 15:50). When the soul remembers again its origin and renounces the body and the material world which is its prison, it will be reunited to its spirit and become once more an angel in Heaven. It was generally held that God had allowed Satan to put the souls of the angels who had rebelled into the bodies he had made in order to give these souls the opportunity of repenting and expiating their fault. Having been purified by suffering they will seek return and thus make amends for their sin and undo the work of Satan. Satan thinks that by this means he will assure his rule over them and detach them for ever from Heaven. He aimed to make the world an eternal hell, but God has tricked him and transformed it into a temporary Purgatory.

The better to assure his dominion Satan passed himself off to the imprisoned angels as God. 'He sat upon the clouds and sent his ministers, even angels flaming with fire, unto man from Adam even unto Enoch his servant.' He is the Jehovah of the Old Testament, angry, vengeful, jealous, so different from the loving Father revealed by Jesus. The Cathars frequently cited his command to sacrifice animals as the clearest proof that the God of the Old Testament was really Satan. 'He began to teach them to perform the custom of sacrifice and unrighteous mysteries, and so did he hide the kingdom of Heaven from men. And he said unto them: "Behold that I am your god and beside me is none other god."'

In order to recall the kingdom of Heaven to man and deliver him from the power of Satan, God sent Christ into the world; 'And therefore did my Father send me into the world that I might make it known unto men, that they might know the evil device of the devil.'

Christ was divine. He was the son of God, as all spirits are in essence, an emanation of the divine quality, but not the transcendent first principle of the Universe. In order, however, to save men from Lucifer he received from the Father 'all power in Heaven and earth', *Vis-a-vis* mankind, therefore, He could be considered as God, God reduced to the measure and stature of a man, a perfect human expression of the divine nature, God in so far as God can be personified. But because He was a pure spirit from the court of God He could not take on a 'body of clay' for that would place Him under the dominion of Satan and He would become merely another imprisoned angel like the rest of mankind.

When my Father thought to send me into the world he sent his angel before me, by name Mary, to receive me. And I when I came down entered in by the ear and came forth by the ear. And Satan, the prince of this world perceived that I was come to seek and to save them that were lost, and sent his angel, even Elias the prophet, baptizing with water: who is called John the Baptist. And Elias asked the prince of this world: How can I know him? Then his lord said: On whomsoever thou shalt see the spirit descending like a dove and resting upon him, he it is that baptizeth with the Holy Ghost unto forgiveness of sins.[2]

From this it follows that Christ had a spiritual or apparent body, and so could not suffer or die corporeally, a view widely held by early Christians. Among the Cathars there seem to have been some differences of opinion on this point, which, like so many others, was not asserted dogmatically. But all were agreed that the essence of Christ's mission to men lay in his teaching and example, in bringing again to the remembrance of men the knowledge of their Heavenly Father and His Kingdom, and showing them how to overcome 'the prince of this world'. He was not an expiatory victim sacrificed to satisfy eternal justice for the redemption of man's sin, but a teacher and elder brother of humanity sent from God to bring the liberating truth to the world. His sufferings, if they were real, were merely the malice of Satan. What should deliver man was not the suffering and death of a Son of God, but the knowledge of man's true origin and destiny. This knowledge and teaching Christ conferred on the Apostles and they in turn on the 'good Christians' who from generation to generation have transmitted it in all its purity and who, moulding their lives after the pattern of that divine example, form the true Church of Christ.

In opposition to this true Church of Christ, Satan, having failed with his first chosen people the Jews, having failed to abort the mission of Christ by sending Elias to precede him and teach the false baptism with water, having stirred up the Jews to reject Christ and slay Him, created the Catholic Church to continue the opposition of the Old Testament to the New, to travesty the Christian Revelation, to persecute the good Christians, and oppose the cult of Satan to the true worship of the spirit.

The Cathars made a profound study of the New Testament and encouraged their Credents to study it too, making for their benefit numerous translations in the vulgar tongue. They claimed its support for their views, and in their debates with the Catholics they could align an impressive number of texts in their support, such as St Paul's distinction of the natural and spiritual bodies (1 Cor. 15) and of the 'house not made with hands, eternal in the Heavens' in contrast to 'this tabernacle in which we groan' (2 Cor. 5). Christ came to 'save that which was lost' (Matt. 18:11) and to redeem 'the lost sheep of the house of Israel' (Matt. 15:24), by which the heavenly people are represented, and 'He preached to the spirits that are in prison' (1 Peter 3:19).

But the Cathars specially reverenced the Gospel of St John as the intimate revelation of Jesus Christ to the one disciple who above all understood Him. The whole tenour of this Gospel, and particularly the discourse at the Last Supper, fits the Catharist view in a manner which cannot fail to strike the impartial reader:

'I testify of the world that the works thereof are evil.' (7:7)

'Ye [the Jews] are of this world, I am not of this world' (8:23)

'The prince of this world is judged' (16:11)

'My kingdom is not of this world' (18: 36)

'Ye [His disciples] are not of the world, but I have chosen you out of the world.'

'I pray not for the world but for them which Thou hast given me, for they are thine' (17: 9)

'They are not of the world even as I am not of the world' (17: 16)

The Cathars rejected by contrast the Old Testament as the work of Satan. Here they were faced with the problem that the Old Testament is frequently quoted in the New, and the arguments by which they got over this difficulty were somewhat weaker. As Satan was pretending to be God he had to put in some good material to sustain the part. On other occasions the spirit of God was able to slip in unawares when a prophet was under the inspiration of Satan, and again, even before the coming of Christ the prophets occasionally remembered something of 'that imperial palace whence they came'. By such arguments they justified a relative acceptance of some of the Old Testament books, notably the Prophets and the Psalms. Of the latter they quoted Psalm 142: 7: 'Bring my soul out of prison that I may praise Thy name.'

Such a conception of the Universe and man's place in it had practical consequences which the Cathars applied with rigorous logic and which, then and now, have caused them to be denounced as enemies of society. They believed that when a man had at last come to realize his true condition as a fallen angel imprisoned in the flesh he must entirely renounce the material world and all that binds him to it in order to be reunited to his holy spirit and become again an angel in Heaven. When he felt ready to take this step he underwent a long probation of fasting and self-discipline and then asked for the Consolamentum or baptism of the Spirit. This was conferred by the laying on of hands with prayer by other Cathars. Thenceforth he was purified of matter, clean, *Katharos* (John 13:10–11), like the disciples of Christ, and was called a 'good man' or 'good Christian'. By this ceremony his soul was not only liberated from its 'filthy carnal envelope' but was reunited to the spirit it had left behind in Heaven.

The good man was once more an angel and as such an object of veneration to his fellow-men, among whom he moved like another Christ. But if he had achieved the privileges of Christhood he had also incurred the obligation to live like Christ and to devote himself entirely to the salvation of his fellows still in prison. His renunciation of the world must be entire, his observance of all the precepts of the Gospel absolute, and he must imitate Christ in His suffering and death if need be. There was no conception among the Cathars, once their own liberation had been attained, of turning their backs on the world and enjoying their blessedness in contemplative isolation. It was their sacred duty to work for the redemption of their fellows from the thrall of Satan by setting an example of unwavering devotion after the pattern set by the Divine Exemplar.

On receiving the Consolamentum the good Christian was obliged to take a number of solemn engagements. He must never shed blood and must henceforth abstain from all animal food, including eggs and milk. This was due to their belief in the inherent evil of propagation as the means whereby Satan had imprisoned the angels in bodies of clay, which bodies are his work and cannot therefore serve as nourishment for one who has thrown off his fetters. Fish was, however, excepted from this prohibition owing to the medieval belief that fish do not reproduce sexually. The good Christian must also take a vow of perpetual virginity. There could be no question that, having liberated himself from the flesh and dedicated himself to the liberation of others, he should then commit the act which draws down other spirits into the prison of the flesh. If married, therefore, he must renounce his wife, though it was prescribed that she must give her consent to this. Henceforth he must never so much as touch a woman. In obedience to the Gospel he must never lie and never swear an oath. This latter prohibition made them seem anarchists in feudal society which was bound together by oaths. Finally, they must never betray their faith in the face of any menace whatever. They understood betraying the faith to be not so much a recantation as any failure to live in strict accordance with the life of a good Christian.

In addition to these solemn engagements the good Christian was obliged to subject himself to the very severe regime which was customarily practised among the Cathars. He must abandon all his material possessions and live in common with the other Cathars. To avoid the temptations of the flesh he must never sleep unclothed and must never travel without a companion. He must also observe three annual fasts of six weeks each, during which he lived on bread and water only for the first and last weeks and for three days in each of the other weeks.

Such was the life of the good Christian, the Perfect Cathar, at the end of which he was assured of final deliverance from the bond of Satan and of returning to his place in Heaven. But such a life could only be for the few, for a spiritual élite. Those who found it impossible to achieve so stern and exalted a virtue accorded their reverence to the good men, listened to their teaching, believed in their doctrine, strove as best they could to lead more Christian lives, and nourished the hope that one day they would be worthy to receive the Consolamentum. If they died without receiving it they would reincarnate in another body and so continue until they were ready for liberation. If, however, at their death, they repented of their sins and undertook the obligations of a good Christian, they might receive the Consolamentum and so be saved from the 'bad death' and brought to the 'good end'. The great majority of the initiations recorded are of this kind. Just as the Christians of the third and fourth centuries frequently delayed baptism and the assumption of the obligations of full membership of the Church until they were on their death-beds, so the Catharist Credents adopted the same compromise, enjoying 'the world, the flesh and the devil' during their lives and leaving the salvation of their souls till they were in the article of death. But to receive the Consolamentum it was indispensable to express the desire, and in case they should be incapable of speech at this supreme moment, many Credents undertook in advance to receive the baptism of the spirit at their deaths by a convention known as the Convenientia.

Such death-bed Consolations do not seem, however, to have had the same validity as those taken in full health. The latter were accorded only after a long and rigorous probation. The candidate had to quit his family and live in common with the Cathars, sharing their lives and participating to the full in their regime for at least two years. Even then he might be rejected if considered unworthy or incapable of sustaining the life to which he aspired. This initiation was more like an ordination admitting to a priesthood and required a genuine vocation of the aspirant for although the Catharist Church had its hierarchy of bishops and deacons, all Cathars were regarded as ministers of the Word and equal in spiritual powers. The death-bed Consolation of a Credent, on the other hand, was more like Extreme Unction. While it was essentially the same ceremony, the ritual was abridged according to the circumstances and it was refused only if the Credent, not having made his Convenientia, were unable to ask for it, or if his death did not appear to be imminent. In the event of his recovery after receiving the Consolamentum it was laid down that he must apply to be consoled again. Whether a death-bed Consolamentum was considered to ensure for its recipient the same spiritual advantages of permanent delivery from the world and immediate entry into Heaven it is impossible to declare with certainty. The Catharists often used the expression 'the way of the stars' as a metaphor for death, and we have several references to their belief that certain souls, while liberated from this world, the lowest and furthest removed from heaven, migrated from star to star until they were sufficiently purified to enter Heaven. It seems probable that this was seen to be the lot of the Credent who received the Consolamentum on his death-bed.

For the 'consoled' Cathar, therefore, death was no longer to be dreaded but, on the contrary, 'a consummation devoutly to be wished'. In later times, when persecution had become severe, the custom grew up of deliberately anticipating it with the 'Endura'. This was a voluntary death which was generally accomplished by fasting, though other more drastic means were occasionally employed. Some writers have spoken of the Endura as though it had always been customary and considered as meritorious by the Cathars. In fact there is no mention of it prior to the Inquisition records of the early fourteenth century, and there can be little doubt that it was a practice which developed only as a result of persecution. A consoled Cathar, knowing that Heaven awaited him if he died, whereas to continue living was likely to mean facing the dungeons and torture chambers of the Inquisition, could hardly be blamed if he sought to hasten his liberation from a world which he had ample justification for regarding as Satanic. But in the period when Catharism was flourishing and free the aspirant who sought the Consolamentum did so because he ardently desired to follow in the footsteps of Christ and devote his life to the spreading of the Word. To seek a premature release from the world would be to deny the divine Master he had sworn to follow and to abandon his fellow-men in their darkness like the bad shepherd of the Gospel. On the other hand, it is not improbable that occasionally a simple Credent, having received the Consolamentum on what he supposed to be his death-bed and then finding himself recovering, should hesitate before the choice of strictly observing the austere life of the 'Pure' or compromising a salvation already assured, and might be tempted to consummate a death to which he had already resigned himself. But to say, as some writers have done, that every inducement was made to a sick man who had been consoled to end his life is a gross exaggeration, and we should do well in this connection to recall the words of Réville: 'What we must above all beware of . . . is the tendency of such judges and historians, themselves partial, to present as absolute dogmas, as beliefs positively affirmed by the Cathars, many ridiculous or repugnant eccentricities which were only deductions, real or claimed, from principles they admitted.'

The same caution should be extended to other allegations made by enemies of the period in the heat of conflict and repeated by partisan historians ever since, such as that the Credents were permitted, and even encouraged, by the Perfecti to indulge in every form of vice and loose living on the grounds that (their bodies being Satanic) no harm could come to their souls by the abuse of what was already but a soiled vesture soon to be abandoned to the Satanic elements to which it belonged, while the soul could always be assured of Heaven by a death-bed Consolation. This sort of criticism is on a level with that sometimes made by ignorant Protestants who allege that a Catholic can permit himself any sin and wash it away in the Confessional. In every age and in every religion the hypocritical and the pleasure-loving have contrived to find excuses for their conduct by ingenious sophistries deduced from the principles of the faith they professed, and it would indeed be surprising were Catharism, which captured the adherence of a warm-blooded, passionate, and voluptuous population, an exception to this rule.

There is, however, a certain amount of documentary support for the criticism that for such Credents as aspired to a full Consolamentum the Cathars not only discouraged them from marrying, which was natural, but tolerated that they should keep a mistress in preference to a wife, since this relationship would be more easily broken when the aspirant felt ready to undertake the pure life. Such an attitude might in our day be considered a charitable concession to human frailty, both logical and reasonable if the Cathars denied the sanctity of marriage. On this point the scanty evidence available is inconclusive. In the Book of John it is written: 'The disciples of John marry and are given in marriage, but my disciples neither marry nor are given in marriage, but are as the angels of God in Heaven. But I said: if then it be sin to have to do with a woman it is not good to marry. And the Lord said unto me: Not everyone can receive this saying', and he goes on to quote Matthew 19: 11–12 on those who have made themselves eunuchs for the kingdom of Heaven's sake. Marriage was certainly tolerated for the Credents, but equally certainly it was not a sacrament. It is not possible to be more specific on the available evidence.

There were a number of matters of faith and practice in which the Cathars, in common with the Revivalist movements of the period, differed emphatically from Catholicism. They abhorred the cult of saints and their relics: saints were in Heaven and liberated from the world, their relics were the very bonds of Satan which by their virtues they had cast off. The Mass was error throughout for Christ never had a physical body and never could have, while bread is matter and therefore the antithesis of the spirit. Sacraments administered by an unworthy priest they held to be of no value, Holy Orders could confer no automatic validity, only the goodness of his life could give supernatural virtue to a priest.

On the strength of such coincidences many Protestant writers have been tempted to seek in Catharism a forerunner of Protestantism. Nothing could be further from the truth. Catharism is 'a direct and authentic continuation of a vast religious current'. It is the fruit of an organic growth whose roots lie far back in the early centuries of Christianity. Its theology was the result of its own tradition and development and was not called into being by scholars and reformers protesting against the corruption of contemporary Christianity and harking consciously back to the infancy of the Church in search of the pure stream. In all essential points Catharism is as strongly opposed to Protestant as to Catholic theology. If, for example, the Cathars rejected the doctrine of forgiveness of sins by the merits of Christ and the saints they equally emphatically rejected the theory of salvation by grace, since the Redemption was not for them an expiation. If they rejected the Mass because bread, being matter, had no sacramental value, they rejected baptism in water for the same reason. They condemned not merely the idolatry of the Cross but rejected it as a symbol, holding it in abhorrence as the instrument upon which Satan sought to torture the Christ.

Differences such as these may be considered of only academic interest and esteemed creditable or otherwise to the Cathars according to individual belief and prediliction. A more serious matter to the modern mind is the charge that the logical consequence of Catharist doctrine could only be the voluntary extinction of the human species. Defenders of Catharism have of course not failed to point out that celibacy was prescribed only for the few and that Catholicism equally demands celibacy of its priests and accords a superior sanctity to the voluntary celibacy of the monk and the nun. It is hardly necessary to say that this is no real answer to the charge, for Catholicism, at the price perhaps of a logical inconsistency, maintained that celibacy would always be restricted to an élite, while for the mass of mankind 'increase and multiply' is a divine command. For the Cathars, on the other hand, 'increase and multiply' is the command of Satan, the means by which he secures his dominion over the soul of man. That strict celibacy should in practice be confined to an élite was for them a temporary and imperfect state of affairs which would come to an end as soon as the mass of mankind had been brought to the realization of its true state. Their logical ideal could only be a world of 'Good Christians' which, as soon as it was achieved would mean no world at all so far as the human race is concerned.

Logically this is unanswerable. In practice we have seen that, although the Cathars considered procreation to be a Satanic act, they also believed that God had permitted Satan to imprison the souls of the fallen angels in bodies in order to afford them the opportunity of repenting and purging their fault, which was indispensable to their salvation. And if the angels are as the stars for multitude, the extinction of the human race as a consequence of its strict application of Catharist principles is an event likely to be as remote as the orthodox Day of Judgement.

For all practical purposes, then, this argument is puerile. Both Catholic and Cathar were agreed that man lives in an imperfect and transitory world where he feels himself 'a stranger and a pilgrim', that above and beyond it is a more perfect state to which he really belongs and to which he can aspire, that an all-wise and loving Providence is the source and guide of all, and that man's present unhappy and imperfect condition must be due to some original sin or fall from grace. These premises arise from deep wells of intuition within the human race. Upon these

> High instincts before which our mortal nature
> Did tremble like a guilty thing surprised

man has pored with clumsy intellect, raising vast edifices of logic and theology which are no more than ephemeral excrescences, built with the intellectual bricks of the period which gives them birth, helpful and satisfying in the atmosphere of their time, but finally cumbering the divine ground on which they stand. The plain truth is that both orthodox and Catharist theologies are equally out of date. A comparison between them should be no more than an academic curiosity. If the two be compared with the dispassionate appraisal accorded to museum pieces the impartial modern mind may be disposed to agree that the comparison is by no means to the disadvantage of Catharism, whether considered as ethics, as philosophy, or as mere common sense.

Orthodoxy accuses the Cathars of dualism. Does it not itself profess a dualism more fundamental and more intolerable? The Cathars, though they postulated a Creator of the material world in opposition to God, yet believed that all souls were divine and would eventually return to Heaven, even Satan himself, so that at the consummation the divine unity will be complete. Its dualism is provisional and temporary. But orthodoxy, if it starts with the divine unity—and yet it too admits the existence of Satan—would end the cosmic process in a dualism which is eternal, the everlasting separation of the blessed in Heaven and the damned in Hell. Catharism rejected the doctrine of Hell and Purgatory. For them this world is the only place of suffering in the universe, and it is not eternal, its existence is a mere temporary aberration.

Both Cathars and orthodox are agreed in seeking the explanation of man's present condition in an original sin of which he is now suffering the consequences. But instead of imputing this original sin to one man, by whose fault all his descendants are under a curse, the Cathars held that each individual soul had sinned in Heaven before the creation of the world when it elected freely to follow Satan in his revolt, and that the world itself in its imperfection is the result of that sin. And just as they rejected a collective condemnation of humanity for one man's sin, so they rejected a collective and vicarious salvation by one man's offering of himself as a sacrificial victim to satisfy the divine Justice. They believed that each soul would find its own salvation when it remembered again its origin and renounced its bondage to the world by receiving the baptism of the Holy Spirit and living the life of a 'Good Christian'.

What shall we say of orthodox eschatology, of the catastrophic Day of Judgment impending at every moment, 'coming like a thief in the night' at the will of a force outside man and judging him irrevocably in one unpredictable instant? Catharism at least placed it in man's own power, as himself a portion of the divine nature, to achieve his salvation in his own time, and did not leave him, whatever his merits and efforts, a mere helpless pawn in the cosmic drama.

Catharism always looked beyond the temporal to the things which are unseen and eternal. It abhorred the cult of relics and had a clean and wholesome attitude to death. Once the soul had set out on the way of the stars the discarded body was treated as a soiled vesture and disposed of decently but without ceremony or regret. There could be for them no morbid cult of tombs and graveyards and the Resurrection of the Body was a Satanic conception.

Theology may be only the intellectual wrapping round the religious urge of the divine spirit in man, but while in our day orthodox Christianity is in danger of being stifled in its wrappings, Catharism still has a message of value to our times: their conception of the redemptive mission of Christ as a sermon rather than an expiation, as an example for the Christian to follow in his life rather than a mystery to be believed by faith. Catharism can bring us this message with the highest warrants, for it speaks with apostolic authority. It reveals to us a genuine and primitive Christian tradition independent of the orthodoxy which has prevailed, a condition in which those characteristic doctrines which have today become a stumbling-block and which are repulsing people from Christ in their millions—original sin, vicarious atonement, eternal damnation, the Day of Judgement, the resurrection of the flesh—have no place. We shall endeavour to show in our conclusion that the branch of the Christian tradition which Catharism represents is better adapted to serve as the foundation for a Christianity which can meet the needs of the modern world.

9

Ritual and Affiliation

THERE were five distinctive rites characteristic of Catharism: the Blessing of Bread, the Melioramentum, the Apparelhamentum or Confession, the Kiss of Peace, and the Consolamentum or Baptism of the Spirit.

Cathars and Credents made a frequent practice of taking a meal in common. These meals began with a solemn blessing of the bread by one of the Cathars, who then recited over it the Lord's Prayer, broke it, and distributed it to all present. After this 'Bread of the Orison' had been eaten the ordinary meal followed.

The Melioramentum is always referred to by Catholic writers as the adoration of the Perfecti. It was the custom at the termination of any ceremony or meeting, or indeed whenever a Credent met a Cathar, for the Credent to make three genuflexions with head bowed and hands joined asking the blessing of the Cathars in these terms: 'Good Christians, give us God's blessing and yours. Pray to the Lord for us that God will preserve us from the bad death and bring us to the good end and to the hands of faithful Christians.' The Cathar answers: 'God bless you and keep your soul from the bad death and bring you to the good end.'

There were slight variations in the wording, but the sense was always the same. By the bad death was meant to die while still under the bondage of Satan and therefore subject to reincarnation, while the good end meant to have received the Consolamentum and thus to be liberated for ever from the flesh at death. By this rite the Credent affirmed that he accepted the Cathar faith, recognized the superior sanctity of the Cathars, and hoped himself to receive the Consolamentum one day. The Inquisition regarded it as an infallible sign of a Credent if he had ever 'adored' the Cathars. It should be mentioned that the 'adoration' was not for the man, but for the Holy Spirit incarnate in him.

The Apparelhamentum was a general confession made as a rule

91

once a month in set terms. The formula was, according to the Lyon ritual:

We have come before God and before you and before the ordinances of Holy Church that we may receive pardon and penance for all our sins in thought word and deed from our birth until now and we ask of God mercy and of you that you pray for us to the Holy Father of Mercy that He forgive us.

Let us worship God and declare all our sins and numerous offences in the sight of the Father, the Son and the honoured Holy Spirit, of the honoured Holy Gospels and the honoured Holy Apostles, by prayer and faith and by the salvation of all the upright and glorious Christians and blessed ancestors asleep and the brethren here present, for their sake we ask you, holy lord, to pardon all our sins. Benedicite, parcite nobis. For numerous are the sins by which we daily offend God, night and day, in thought, word and deed, wittingly and unwittingly, and especially by the desires that evil spirits bring to us in the flesh which clothes us. Benedicite, parcite nobis.

Whereas we are taught by God's Holy word as well as by the Holy Apostles and the preaching of our spiritual brothers to reject all fleshly desire and all uncleanness and to do the will of God by doing good we, unworthy servants that we are, not only do not do the will of God as we should, but more often give way to the desires of the flesh and the cares of the world, to such an extent that we wound our spirits. Benedicite, parcite nobis. We go with those who are of the world, mixing with them, talking and eating with them, and sinning in many things so that we wound our brothers and our spirits. Benedicite, parcite nobis. By our tongues we fall into idle words, vain talk, mockery and malice, detraction of our brothers and sisters whom we are not worthy to judge nor to condemn their faults. Among Christians we are sinners. Benedicite, parcite nobis. The penance which we received we have not observed as we ought to have done, neither the fasting nor the prayer. We have wasted our days and hours. While we are saying the Holy Prayer our senses are diverted to carnal desires and worldly cares, so that at this moment we hardly know what we can offer to the Father of the Just. Benedicite, parcite nobis.

This confession was made in public by all together and there does not seem to have been any form of particular confession of individual faults. The penance imposed was also general and usually consisted of three days' fasting on bread and water and the recitation of the Lord's Prayer a set number of times.

All ceremonies and meetings ended with the Kiss of Peace. The Cathars kissed each of the Credents on both cheeks and the Credents exchanged the kiss among themselves in the same way, men with men and women with women. Since, however, the Cathars must never touch a woman, the Kiss of Peace was transmitted to them by the leading Cathar kissing the Gospel, which was afterwards kissed by one of the women present, who then transmitted the kiss in the normal manner to the other women.

The most important of all Cathar ceremonies was the Consolamentum, the Baptism of the Spirit by which the Credent was admitted to membership of the Church and became a Good Christian. These alone possessed the truth and virtue which Christ conveyed to His Apostles and which had been transmitted solely by the intermediary of the Cathars. The Consolamentum is at once baptism, absolution, and ordination. The essence of it is the communication of the Holy Spirit by the laying on of hands. But the Holy Spirit thus received was not conceived by the Cathars as that of the Trinity. It was rather that individual portion of the Holy Spirit from which the soul had been separated at its fall into matter which was now restored to the soul at its liberation from the bondage of matter.

The preparation for the Consolamentum was like that for Baptism in the early Church. The candidate was carefully prepared and instructed as the Catechumens had been. This period was called the Abstinentia and lasted at least twelve months, often two years. Even this was preceded by a period of probation and observation lasting for one or two years. The postulant had to quit his family and live in common with the Cathars, sharing their manner of life and owing them absolute obedience.

At the end of this period came the Traditio, the actual ceremony, preceded by the delivery of the Prayer. This was usually held in public and before a considerable congregation. On all the walls many candles and torches were lit as a symbol of the baptism by fire. In the centre was a table covered with a white linen cloth on which lay the New Testament. The postulant stood before the table, while the Cathars, having washed their hands, assembled in a circle. The officiating Cathar then addressed the postulant in these words:

[. . .] you must realize that when you are before the Church of God you are before the Father, the Son and the Holy Ghost, as the Scriptures teach. For Christ said in the Gospel according to St Matthew, 'Wheresoever two or three are gathered together in my name there I am in the midst of them.' And in the Gospel according to St. John he said, 'If a man love me he will keep my words, and my Father will love him, and we will come unto him and make our abode with him.' And St. Paul says in the Second Epistle to the Corinthians, 'Ye are the Temple of the living God, as God hath said by Isaiah, "I will dwell in them and walk in them; and I will be their God, and they shall be My people. Wherefore come out from among them and be ye separate, saith the Lord; and touch not the unclean thing; and I will receive you, and will be a Father unto you, and ye shall be My sons and daughters, saith the Lord Almighty."' And in another place he says, 'Seek ye the proof of Christ Who speaketh in me.' And in the First Epistle to Timothy he says, 'These things write I unto thee, hoping to come unto thee shortly; but if I tarry long, that thou mayest know how thou oughtest to behave thyself in the House of God, which is the Church of the Living God, the pillar and ground of the truth.' And he said also to the Hebrews, 'But Christ is as a Son over His own house, Whose house we are.'

That the Spirit of God is with the followers of Jesus Christ, Christ has shown thus in the Gospel according to St John, 'If ye love me, keep my commandments. And I will pray the Father, and He shall give you another Comforter, that He may abide with you forever; even the Spirit of Truth, Whom the world cannot receive, because it seeth Him not, neither knoweth Him; but ye know Him, for He dwelleth with you, and shall be in you. I will not leave you comfortless, I will come to you.' And in the Gospel according to St Matthew He said, 'Lo, I am with you alway, even unto the end of the world.' And St Paul said in the First Epistle to the Corinthians, 'Know ye not that ye are the Temple of God, and that the Spirit of God dwelleth in you? If any man defile the temple of God, him shall God destroy; for the Temple of God is holy, which temple ye are.' Christ shows it thus in the Gospel according to St Matthew, 'For it is not ye that speak but the Spirit of your Father that speaketh in you.' And St John says in his epistle, 'By this we know that we abide in Him and He in us, for He has given us of His Spirit.' And St Paul said to the Galatians, 'Because ye are sons God hath sent forth the spirit of His Son into your hearts, crying, "Father! Father!"'

Wherefore be it understood that your presentation made before the sons of Jesus Christ confirms the faith and teaching of the Church of God as the Holy Scriptures tell us. For in former times the people of God separated themselves from the Lord their God. And they abandoned the will and guidance of their Heavenly Father through the deceptions of wicked spirits and by submission to their will. And for these reasons, and many others, we are certain that the Heavenly Father would have pity on His people and receive them again in peace and concord by the coming of His Son, Jesus Christ, and now is the time. For you are here before the disciples of Jesus Christ in the place where Father, Son and Holy Ghost have their spiritual abode as is shown above, to receive that Holy Prayer which the Lord Jesus gave to His disciples, so that your prayers might be granted by our Heavenly Father. Therefore must you learn that if you would receive this Holy Prayer you must repent of your sins and forgive all men. For Our Lord Jesus Christ says, 'If ye forgive not men their trespasses, neither will your Heavenly Father forgive your trespasses.'

Hence it is meet that you be resolved in your heart to keep this Holy Prayer all your life according to the custom of the Church of God, in purity and truth, and in all other virtues which God would bestow upon you. Wherefore we pray the good Lord who bestowed upon the disciples of Jesus Christ the virtue to receive this Holy Prayer steadfastly that He may grant to you also the grace to receive it steadfastly, in His honour and for your salvation.

The Elder then said the Lord's Prayer and the postulant followed him phrase by phrase after which the Elder said: 'We deliver you this Holy Prayer that you may receive it of us and of God and of the Church, that you may have the power to say it all your life, day and night, alone or in company, and that you must never eat or drink without first saying it. If you omit to do so you must do penance.' The Postulant replied: 'I receive it of you and of the Church.' Then he made his melioramentum and gave thanks.

Then the Elder asked the postulant, 'My brother, do you desire to give yourself to our faith?'

The Postulant having answered 'Yes', he asked three times, making a bow and advancing one step between each, 'Bless me', to which the Elder replied, 'God bless you.'

At the third time the Postulant added, 'Lord, pray to God for me a sinner that He will lead me to the good end', and the Elder answered: 'God bless you and make you a good Christian and bring you to the good end.'

Elder: Do you give yourself to God and the Gospel?
Postulant: Yes.
Elder: Do you promise that henceforth you will eat neither meat nor eggs, nor cheese, nor fat, and that you will live only from water and wood [i.e. on fish and vegetables] that you will not lie, that you will not swear, that you will not kill, that you will not abandon your body to any form of luxury, that you will never go alone when it is possible to have a companion, that you will never sleep without breeches and shirt and that you will never abandon your faith for fear of water, fire or any other manner of death?
Postulant: Yes.

Then followed the second allocution:

[. . .] you wish to receive the spiritual baptism whereby the Holy Spirit is given in the Church of God with the Holy Prayer by the laying on of hands of the Good Men. Of this Baptism Our Lord Jesus Christ said in the Gospel according to St Matthew, 'Go ye and teach all nations, baptizing them in the Name of the Father and of the Son and of the Holy Ghost; teaching them to observe all things whatsoever I have commanded you; and lo, I am with you always, even unto the end of the world.' And in the Gospel of St Mark he said, 'Go ye into all the world and preach the Gospel to every creature. He that believeth and is baptised shall be saved, but he that believeth not shall be damned.' And in the Gospel of St John He said to Nicodemus, 'Verily, verily I say unto thee, except a man be born of water and the spirit he cannot enter into the kingdom of God.' And John the Baptist spoke of this baptism when he said, 'I indeed baptize you with water, but one mightier than I cometh, the latchet of whose shoes I am not worthy to unloose; he shall baptize you with the Holy Ghost and with fire.' And Jesus Christ said in the Acts of the Apostles, 'John baptized with water but ye shall be baptized with the Holy Ghost.'

This gift of the Holy Spirit by the laying on of hands has been instituted by Jesus Christ as St Luke tells, and he said that his friends would confer it as St Mark says, 'They shall lay hands on the sick and they shall recover.' And Ananias conferred this Baptism on St Paul when he was converted. And afterwards Paul and Barnabas conferred it on the Samaritans. For St Luke says thus in the Acts of the Apostles, 'Now when the Apostles which were at Jerusalem heard that Samaria had received the word of God they sent unto them Peter and John, who when they were come down, prayed for them that they might receive the Holy Spirit, for as yet He was fallen upon none of them.' Then they laid their hands on them and they received the Holy Spirit. This Holy Baptism by which the Holy Spirit is given the Church of God has kept from the Apostles until now, and it has come from the Good Men to the Good Men until now and shall do till the end of the world.'

And you must understand that power is given to the Church of God to bind and to loose, to forgive sins and to retain them, as Christ said in the Gospel of St John, 'As my Father hath sent me, even so send I you. And when he had said this he breathed on them and saith unto them Receive ye the Holy Ghost; whoseoever sins ye remit they are remitted unto them, and whosoever sins ye retain, they are retained.' And in the Gospel of St Matthew he said to Simon Peter, 'I say unto thee that thou art Peter and upon this rock I will build my church, and the gates of hell shall not prevail against it. And I will give unto thee the keys of the kingdom of heaven, and whatsoever thou shalt bind on earth shall be bound in heaven, and whatsoever thou shalt loose on earth shall be loosed in heaven.' And in another place he said to his disciples, 'Verily I say unto you, whatsoever ye shall bind on earth shall be bound in heaven and whatsoever ye shall loose on earth shall be loosed in heaven' and again, 'If two of you shall agree on earth as touching anything that they shall ask, it shall be done for them of my Father which is in Heaven. For wheresoever two or three are gathered together in my name there am I in the midst of them.' And in another place he said, 'Heal the sick, cleanse the lepers, raise the dead, cast out devils.' And in the Gospel of St John he said, 'He that believeth on me, the works that I do shall he do also,' and in the Gospel of St Mark he said 'These signs shall follow them that believe; in my name shall they cast out devils, they shall speak with new tongues, they shall take up serpents, and if they drink any deadly thing it shall not hurt them, they shall lay hands on the sick and they shall recover.' And in the Gospel of St Luke he said 'Behold I give unto you power to tread on serpents and scorpions and over all the power of the enemy and nothing shall by any means hurt you.'

And if you wish to receive this power you must keep all the commandments of Christ and the New Testament according to your ability. And know that He has commanded that man shall not commit adultery or murder or lie, that he must not swear any oath, that he shall not seize nor rob, nor do to others what he would not have done to himself, that man must forgive whoever wrongs him and love his enemies, pray for his detractors and accusers and bless them; and if anyone strike him on one cheek, turn to him the other also, and if anyone takes away his cloak, to leave him his coat also; and that he should neither judge nor condemn, and many other commandments which the Lord made for His Church. Also you must hate this world and its works and the things of this world, for St John says in his epistle, 'O my beloved, love not the world, neither the things that are in the world. If any man love the world the love of the Father is not in him. For all that is in the world, the lust of the flesh and the lust of the eyes and the pride of life, is not of the Father but is of the world. And the world passeth away and the lust thereof, but he that doeth the will of God abideth for ever.' And Christ said unto the Gentiles, 'The world cannot hate you, but me it hates because I bear witness of it that its works are evil.' And in the Book of Solomon it is written, 'I have seen all the

View of Ussat-les-Bains

Ruins of the Chateau de Lordat, 1938

Gadal under the 'Pentagon' in Bethlehem cave

Gadal and the 'Green Osiris'

Antonin Gadal

Left to right:
Rinderknecht,
Gadal,
Walter Birks, 1939

Rinderknecht in the 'Pentagon' (photograph: Hans Steiner)

Bethlehem cave: the 'Birks' wall and gate, erected in 1937

Major Walter Birks MBE, 1945

View of Bethlehem cave at Ussat

Two views of Montségur

Memorial to the Cathars at Montségur

works that are done under the sun, and behold, all is vanity and vexation of spirit.' And Jude the brother of James said for our instruction in his Epistle, 'Hate this soiled garment of the flesh.' And by these witnesses and many others, you must keep the commandments of God and hate the world. And if you continue well to the end, we have the hope that your soul shall have life eternal.'

And the Credent shall say, 'I have this will, pray to God for me that He will give me His power.'

Then one of the Good Men shall make his melioramentum with the Credent to the Elder and say, 'Parcite nobis. Good Christians we pray you by the love of God that you grant this blessing, which God has given you, to our friend here present.' And the Credent shall make his melioramentum and say, 'Parcite nobis. For all the sins I have ever done in thought, word and deed, I ask pardon of God, of the Church and of you all.' And the whole assembly of Cathars shall reply, 'By God and by us and by the Church, may your sins be forgiven and we pray God to forgive you them.'

Then all present recited three times 'Adoremus Patrem, et Filium et Spiritum Sanctam.'

The Postulant was once more reminded of the serious obligations he was undertaking and called upon to renounce his wife, if married (or husband in the case of a woman).

After this followed the parcia. The Postulant knelt and put both hands on the ground saying, 'Bless me' and did this three times, advancing each time but still on the ground. The third time he added, addressing the Elder, 'Lord, pray to God for me, a sinner, that He will lead me to the good end.' The Elder replied, 'God bless you, make you a good Christian and bring you to the good end.'

The Postulant now took his solemn engagement in these words:

I promise to give myself to God and the Gospel, never to lie or swear, never again to touch a woman, to kill no animal and to eat neither meat, nor eggs, nor milk, to live entirely on vegetables and fish, to do nothing without saying the Lord's Prayer, never to travel or pass the night anywhere nor even eat, without a companion; and if I fall into the hands of my enemies and am separated from my brother, to abstain from all food for at least three days, never to sleep unclothed and finally never to betray my faith before any threat of death whatever.

Then the Elder takes the Book, the New Testament, and places it on the postulant's head, while the other good men lay their hands on him saying, 'Holy Father, receive Thy servant into Thy righteousness and put Thy grace and Holy Spirit upon him.' Then all said the Lord's Prayer followed by the Adoremus three times and the Lord's Prayer once more. Then, from the New Testament, open upon the postulant's head, the Elder read the first seventeen verses of St John's Gospel. After three more Adoremus and the Lord's Prayer again, the postulant rose and was clothed in the black robe, the *sadère,* which was the outward mark of the Cathar. In time of persecution this was replaced by a plaited woollen girdle (the *kosti*) worn under the clothes. He was now *hereticus vestitutus,* 'clothed upon, that mortality might be swallowed up in life,' (2 Cor. 5:4) and had 'put on the Lord Jesus Christ' (Romans 13:14).

In the case of a person receiving the Consolamentum on his death bed these rites were abridged and simplified according to the circumstances of the case. The sick man was asked, 'Do you wish to receive the gift of God and the holy ordination which the Lord brought from the Heavenly court to confide to the Apostles and which they transmitted to the good men and so until now?' Unless the sick man had already made his Convenientia, it was indispensable that he should reply affirmatively and *viva voce*. Then he must make his confession as far as he was able. He was required to take the same engagements as for a postulant in full health and the Prayer was delivered to him in the same manner. The New Testament was placed on a clean white cloth on the bed and the laying on of hands proceeded as described above.

All these rites and ceremonies of the Cathars correspond in a most striking manner with those of the primitive Christian Church. In this liturgy of Lyon, written in the Langue d'Oc of the twelfth century, we recover the very atmosphere of the first centuries of Christianity in Asia Minor and Syria, down to the very wording in some cases.

In the first century of the Christian era the Eucharist formed part of a general meal in common known as the *Agape*, or love-feast. But from the very earliest times this practice was found to be liable to lead to abuses, as we can see from St Paul's first letter to the Corinthians (11: 20 ff.) Gradually, therefore, the custom grew up of separating the Eucharist from the Agape in order to give greater solemnity to the former, which, in the religious atmosphere of the Hellenistic period, soon acquired a sacramental character, while the Agape fell into disuse. Already by the time of Justin Martyr, *circa* AD 160, there is no mention of the Agape in connection with the Eucharist. Justin thus describes the eucharistic banquet (*Apologia,* 1.65).

The prayer being finished, bread, wine and water are brought. The president prays and gives thanks as long as he can and the people reply with Amen. A portion of the elements which have been blessed is then distributed to each person and for those who are absent their share is sent to them by the ministry of the deacons.

The Cathar ceremony of a common meal at which the bread was solemnly blessed, broken, and distributed must therefore have been preserved unchanged from a period at least as far back in the history of the church as the middle of the second century. There is also very strong evidence that in the time of the Apostles the bread was blessed by saying the Lord's Prayer over it. The custom of using the words employed by Christ Himself at the Last Supper was a slightly later development which, however, soon displaced the primitive form. In this connection it is interesting to notice that in the Lord's Prayer, which held a position of absolute pre-eminence among the Cathars, the words *Ton arton ton Epiousion* were translated *panem supersubstantialem* and not *panem quotidianum* as has become the orthodox usage. In effect the Greek word *Epiousios* means literally 'for tomorrow' and in praying to God 'Give us tomorrow's bread today' it was felt that this could not refer to material nourishment, but must mean 'the heavenly bread' of which Jesus promised: 'he that eateth of this bread shall live for ever' (John 6: 58).

The Kiss of Peace, which is still preserved at the close of the Catholic Mass, transmitted from the celebrant to his assistants and thence to the congregation, is a very ancient Christian usage which in the Early Church was always associated with the Agape.

The practice of confessing sins publicly in the presence of the whole body of Christians was also the custom of the early Church. The formula appropriate to it is still preserved in the Confiteor of the Mass where the penitent confesses to God, the angels, the saints, and the whole Church, asking them all to join him in praying God for his pardon, and the whole congregation replies, '*Misereatur tui, omnipotens Deus, et demissis peccatis tuis, perducat te ad vitam aeternam.*' The wording throughout shows the very close kinship which exists between the Catholic Confiteor and the Catharist Apparelhamentum.

Even the Melioramentum, at first sight peculiar to the Cathars and sometimes criticized as almost idolatrous, is paralleled in the liturgy of the Mass where the deacon, before reading the Gospel, genuflects to the celebrant asking his blessing. This, too, is clearly a survival of a very ancient Christian usage of which the Catharist Melioramentum is a development.

In the early centuries of the Christian Church there was an intermediate class between those believers who, after a period of instruction and testing known as the catechumenate, had received baptism and formally renounced paganism in order to observe the Christian way of life in every particular, and the mass of pagans who remained completely indifferent or hostile to Christianity. This intermediate category consisted of persons who were sympathetic to Christianity, believed in it, and intended to become Christians, but were unwilling for the time being to give up the customs and mode of life which Christianity condemned, and who usually waited till they were on their death-beds to ask for baptism and thus erase the errors of their lives and assure their salvation. The first Christian Emperors as well as the great mass of their more worldly subjects were Christians of this class, which corresponds exactly to the Catharist Credents. They deferred baptism until their deaths, when it was conferred summarily without the usual preliminary tests and instruction.

But those who desired baptism while still in full health had to submit to a severe noviciate as catechumens. They had first to be 'elected' by the leaders of the Church; that is to say, accepted as suitable. Then, because they had up to that moment been under the dominion of Satan, the demons were driven out of them by an exorcism. They were marked with a cross on the forehead and salt was put on their tongues. Then they were put in charge of catechists who instructed them in Christian doctrine, and on fixed days they were examined on their progress. During these examinations they prostrated themselves before the exorcists who marked them with the cross. Finally they were presented to the priest or bishop for the laying on of hands.

By the thirteenth century these rites had long disappeared from the Church and it had been completely forgotten that they had ever existed. In its baptismal ceremony the medieval Church had telescoped and combined a number of rites formerly distinct. But all these rites are found in the Consolamentum. The Abstinentia, which lasted for at least a year, corresponded to the catechumenate, and during it the candidate had frequently to make his melioramentum to the Cathar who had him in his particular charge, exactly as the catechumens did to the exorcists who examined them.

At the third examination of the catechumens the Gospels and the Lord's Prayer were solemnly delivered.

The elect having been asked to stand and be attentive and respectful, one of the deacons read the first pages of St Matthew. The priest at once added a short commentary. Then the same was done for the other three Gospels. Then came the delivery of the Pater, the supreme prayer which the Lord had Himself taught to His Apostles and through them to all mankind. The priest recited the Lord's Prayer phrase by phrase commenting the text as he went. The last petition having been said and expounded, he ended the ceremony of the traditio with a final address. In their turn the catechumens recited the Pater. Henceforth they could pray as God meant them to.[1]

Before the solemn act by which the catechumens at their seventh examination renounced Satan, his works, and his pomp, the early liturgies of the Eastern Church place an allocution by the priest which was a last reminder of the doctrine which the neophytes were to profess and an exhortation on the obligations they were about to undertake. This usage was still preserved in medieval times in the Monophysite Churches of Antioch, Alexandria, and Edessa. This address we find in the Catharist Consolamentum, while in the ordination ceremony of our own day there is an address to the ordinands in which the bishop defines the attributions of the Order to be conferred and the virtues and graces it demands.

There is a gap in the Cathar ritual at the point corresponding to that in the early Church where the catechumen renounced Satan and his works and pomp. Sacchoni informs us they renounced the faith and baptism of Rome. If so, this would be a later emendation to meet contemporary conditions. After this renunciation the catechumens were baptised in water to wash away original sin and then they asked the bishop for confirmation, which was conferred by the laying on of hands to confer the Holy Spirit. It is to be noted that this supreme initiation had to be asked for.

The final stages of the Consolamentum correspond to the orthodox Ordination, as its earlier stages to. the other three sacraments of Absolution, Baptism, and Confirmation. The laying on of hands by the consecrating bishop and his assistant priests at the ordination of a priest is the most ancient practice of the Church, and of all the rites connected with the consecration of bishops the one which goes back to the primitive Church is that of the Gospel open on the candidate's head. The vesting of the newly-initiated Cathar also corresponds to the Ordination ceremony where the bishop vests the sub-deacon, deacon, or priest with the sacred vestment of the order which has been conferred. The Kiss of Peace, too, figures in the ceremonies of Ordination and Consecration.

These remarkable and detailed correspondences between Cathar ritual and ceremonies and those of early Christianity present us with a problem of far-reaching importance. How came it that sectaries denounced as heretics by the Catholic Church should be found in thirteenth-century Languedoc to have employed a whole liturgy which bears every mark of having been transmitted intact from the infancy of the Church? Any theory of plagiarism or conscious reconstruction of early Christian forms by the Cathars can be ruled out at once, for in the twelfth and thirteenth centuries the historical knowledge which would have been required to reproduce primitive Christianity did not exist. The points of correspondence in the contemporary Catholic liturgy and practice have either dropped out altogether or are mere vestigial survivals, or have been developed along different lines from their point of departure in the common original. It is only with the historical knowledge of our own day that the full significance of the Cathar liturgy can be appreciated, and it can only have reached them by direct transmission from at least as early as the third century, and more probably the second.

Must we then accept the Cathars' own claim to be the true Church of Christ with the only valid Apostolic Succession handed down in unbroken continuity 'from the good men to the good men until now'? And was it therefore the true Church of Christ which was exterminated by the swords of the Crusaders and the stakes of the Inquisition?

If this is the case, what are we to say of the Cathar doctrine and theology which we have described above? Was this after all the true Christian faith? Here we are faced with another difficulty. If the correspondence between the Cathar ritual and the rites of early Christianity is striking, its contrast with the theology imputed to them is no less so. Not only is there throughout the liturgy absolutely no hint of dualism, docetism, reincarnation, or any of the distinctive doctrines attributed to the Cathars, there are many things which would seem to be in direct contradiction, or at least seriously inconsistent with Cathar ideas. In the ceremony of the Apparelhamentum, for example, there is a reference to 'the salvation of all the upright and glorious Christians and the blessed ancestors *asleep*'. They have not then shed the prison of the flesh to set out upon the Way of the Stars, but are awaiting the judgement in their mortal bodies. We have seen that the Cathars rejected Baptism in water and retained only the laying on of hands. Yet in the allocution they retain a quotation from John 3: 'Except a man be born of *water* and the spirit he cannot enter into the kingdom of God', and immediately afterwards they quote John the Baptist, whom they are supposed to have regarded as a demon. Moreover, before conferring the Consolamentum the Cathars all washed their hands in water. In the numerous references to the Holy Spirit there is no hint that it was considered to be individual to the Cathar or other than that of the Trinity. The commission to Peter is stressed and there are quotations from Isaiah and Ecclesiastes and other parts of the Old Testament.

It is true that when we are dealing with the Lyon ritual we are dealing with an original Cathar source, whereas our reconstruction of Catharist theology depends upon the testimony of hostile witnesses and the documents of the Inquisition. But even after making every allowance for distortion, bias, and misrepresentation, the evidence is far too strong to allow us to say that the Lyon ritual alone must be followed and the contemporary Catholic testimony disallowed. Moreover, there is the Book of John, which is equally a Cathar source.

The only possible conclusion is that Catharism embodies a traditional deposit of great age and sanctity which was handed down unchanged, although the theology which accompanied it evolved under the influences surrounding it. Has not orthodoxy followed the same path, modifying primitive Christianity in accordance with western and Roman ideas instead of eastern and Persian ones? But whereas the tradition which has become recognized as orthodox modified its rites and liturgy to keep pace with the evolution of its ideas, the Catharist tradition preserved the early formulas with jealous care from age to age, interpreting its phrases in a new sense as their ideas evolved beyond its literal meaning. What is important for us is to distinguish between Catharism as it actually existed in the twelfth and thirteenth centuries and the tradition which it had preserved. This is a genuine Christian tradition, independent of orthodoxy and reaching back to the Apostles themselves. Catharism and the other links in the chain of succession are merely the surface manifestations of an inner current. The importance of the Cathars, the Bogomils, the Paulicians, and other links in this chain, is not in what can be learned of these sects as to their doctrines, organization, and the rest: such details are even misleading, being in themselves distortions and corruptions, throw-offs due to the inevitable tendency to organize churches and sects with a systematic ideology and teaching acceptable to the masses. The sects decay and die. But they are the spoor which enables us to track our quarry through the centuries. This quarry is the true message of Christianity, the Quest of the Holy Grail, the Imitation of Christ.

The affiliation of the Cathars of Languedoc with the Bogomils of the Balkans and, through them, to the Paulicians of Asia Minor is thoroughly documented by Steven Runciman in *The Medieval Manichee*[2] (1947) and by Arnold Toynbee in *A Study of History* (1939, vol. IV). It needs, therefore, only the briefest recapitulation here.

The Paulicians are first noticed in eastern Asia Minor in the seventh century, in the chaotically fluctuating border area where the new Islamic Empire of the Caliphs was expanding at the expense of both the Christian Byzantines and the Zoroastrian Persians. Of their reputed founder, Constantine Silvanus, Gibbon says: 'the remnant of the Gnostic sects, and especially the Manichaeans of Armenia were united under his standard . . . he preached with success in the regions of Pontus and Cappadocia which had long since imbibed the religion of Zoroaster.' Since the Paulicians strongly condemned images, the iconoclast Byzantine emperors of the eighth century were inclined to be sympathetic towards them and Constantine V (740–75) deliberately settled many of them in Thrace around the city of Philippopolis (Plovdiv) in order to form a protective shield against barbarian incursions into the Balkans. The triumph of the iconodules, however, led to the persecution of the Paulicians in the ninth century. There followed thirty years of warfare reminiscent of the Albigensian crusade.

When the Paulicians were eventually defeated the Emperor John Zimisces (969–75) forcibly transferred many more of them to the Balkans in order to remove them from the proximity of the Arab

Empire, with which they had allied themselves during the struggle. In their new home, however, they converted many Bulgarians, and from this base they proseletyzed so successfully that by the beginning of the thirteenth century they had established flourishing congregations in Bosnia, Dalmatia, Lombardy and, finally and above all, in Languedoc. 'The substantial identity of the Paulician, the Bogomil and the Cathar faith is not in doubt. The common features are too similar and too numerous to be explained away as fortuitous, and it is clear that we are in the presence of a single religion masquerading under different names in different places.' (Toynbee, *op. cit.* p. 631.)

How far can we trace this back beyond the Paulicians of the seventh century?

Constantine Silvanus and his followers assumed that their name had been derived from the Apostle Paul and, since it was this group which came into collision with the Byzantine Empire, it is the better known historically. But, says Toynbee, 'this Pauline conceit appears to have been peculiar to them and to have been unknown in the earlier home of the Paulician church in the Armenian territories on the other side of the Euphrates.' The name he shows on philological analysis to be derived from a derogatory Armenian diminutive of Paul, and he claims that there is 'positive evidence that they were named after Paul of Samosata' who was Bishop of Antioch in the third century.

Although Runciman throws some doubt on this claim he goes even farther back (*op. cit.* p. 174):

We must seek for the origin of 'Christian' Dualism in the same place and time in which orthodox Christianity was born. The ancestry of the former was more mixed and its theology less accurate, but it was inspired at the start by the same religious feeling. As time went on the differences became definite. The turning point was probably Marcion's organisation of a separate Gnostic Church. From that there could be no retreat. Soon after, when orthodox Christianity triumphed with the aid of Imperial Rome, the Gnostic churches lost touch, and divided into two main streams. The one, the more strictly Dualist or, if you will, the more Manichaean, lingered in Armenia and travelled with Armenian colonists to the Balkans. The other, the Monarchian stream, remained to a greater extent the repository of Gnostic tales and early Christian usages, and, revitalized by an evangelical movement known as Messalianism, itself largely inspired by Montanism, came also to Thrace and to the Balkans. There the two branches joined up again, though each retained its fundamental doctrine, and jointly they swept over Europe.

We must, therefore, go right back to the origins of the Christian Church itself and trace its development from the beginning. We shall show how Christianity was first proclaimed in a Jewish setting and was interpreted and presented by its first adherents in terms of contemporary Hebrew conceptions. Then, as it spread into the Hellenized Gentile world, how it came to be interpreted and presented more and more in terms of the ideas prevailing in that wider and more cosmopolitan setting. We shall notice, too, some of the many ideological tributaries which went to swell the broad stream which was eventually canalized and regulated into the Catholic and Orthodox Church. Finally, we shall examine the evidence for the existence of an alternative Christian tradition, equally Apostolic, but which, over the centuries, has taken some of its colouring from sources less familiar to the ideology of the Western world.

10

The Jewish Setting

THE pious Jew, profoundly impressed by the conception of his nation as the chosen of the Most High, found in the actual facts of its history a continual and incomprehensible disillusionment. That God had deserted his chosen people was unthinkable. Therefore He must be chastising them for their shortcomings, purifying and refining them by suffering so as to make them worthy instruments of His purpose. This is the conception of the second Isaiah and the later prophets, 'the suffering servant, despised and rejected of men', who should afterwards be fit to become 'a light to lighten the Gentiles'. This suffering servant is at first the whole nation of Israel (Is. 44: 21, 49: 3–6). From this developed the idea of a morally regenerated Israel which should then reign over all the nations. But if the material prosperity of the nation was to be restored when they had been redeemed, it was natural to picture this as a restoration also of the Davidic monarchy; 'a rod from the stem of Jesse', a scion of the traditional royal house, should reign over the regenerated nation, and therefore over all the nations. The title Messiah, which means Anointed, and of which Christos is the Greek translation, was not at first applied exclusively to this future Davidic king. It was a general term applied to any person who was in some manner specially marked out by God as having a divine commission. As such it is applied in the Old Testament to Saul, David, Solomon, Jehu, and other kings, including even the heathen Cyrus (Isaiah 45: 1). By the first century BC, however, this title of the Anointed One was becoming specifically confined to the expected deliverer and was acquiring a supernatural colouring from the apocalyptic literature in which it was being identified with that 'Son of Man' who shall be revealed from heaven at the end of the Age. This Messianic expectation assumed different forms in each of the religious and political parties of the nation.

The Sadducees were conservative and cautious, a party of religious and political expediency, prepared to come to terms with the Gentile world and to modify the national and religious exclusiveness of the Jews in order to preserve the physical existence of the nation and the continuance of the Temple worship. They represented the established formal religion centred in the Temple and its ritual. They had little sympathy with popular fervour and the crude Messianic expectations of the people which they feared would merely lead to useless revolutionary agitation and provoke the Romans to 'take away our holy place and nation'. In so far as they shared any Messianic hopes, the Messiah they looked for would be a priest of the line of Aaron and Zadok.

At the other extreme were the Zealots, the revolutionary party, which agitated for revolt and the expulsion of the Gentiles by force. They believed that the God of Israel would surely help His people as He had done in the past. If they put their faith in Him He would smite their enemies and the Messiah would appear as the leader of a successful revolt. This party provoked several abortive rebellions, notably that of Judas of Galilee which is referred to in the fifth chapter of Acts, and eventually gained the upper hand in AD 66 when they headed a general rebellion which ended in the destruction of Jerusalem by Titus in AD 70.

The Pharisees, on the other hand, turned to the Scriptures, wherein the Divine Law was revealed as the essence of the Chosen People's religion. God had set the Jews apart as a holy people, but only on condition that they kept His Covenant and obeyed His commands as He had revealed them in the Scriptures. The supreme duty of the Chosen Race therefore was the study of this Divine Law and its scrupulous application. Then, when Israel had made herself holy, had fitted herself to fulfil her part in the divine purpose, God would fulfil His Covenant and redeem His people from their affliction. The Messiah would then appear to break the heathen yoke and re-establish the throne of David in a purged Jerusalem.

It was the period of exile in Babylon which stimulated the intensive study of the Law and the Prophets as the essence of Jewish religion and changed Israel from a nation to a Faith, a Faith whose characteristic exponents were the Scribes and the Pharisees. It was the work of the Scribes to compile and codify the Law, which was studied incessantly and an enormous development made of it by oral tradition. So many legal niceties came to be involved in its observance that only those who devoted themselves entirely to it, who 'separated themselves'—the Parushim, the Pharisees—could possibly observe it in full. This Law, the Torah, as completed, codified, and expounded by the Scribes was regarded as the unalterable expression of the Divine Will and its observance the whole duty of man. With religion thus reduced to a matter of detailed rules of conduct to be scrupulously obeyed, the well of prophecy dried up. There was no room for further revelation.

The characteristic institution of this new form of Hebrew religion was the synagogue. After the return to Palestine large numbers of Jews remained in Babylonia and a flourishing colony also grew up in Egypt under the protection of the Ptolemies. This is the origin of the Diaspora, and this new institution, representing the Pharisaic type of religion, corresponded to the changed circumstances.

Before the Exile the religion of the people of the countryside had been centred upon the numerous local shrines on the 'high places'. Since this form of worship easily became tainted with heathenish practices it was continually denounced by the prophetic school, and Josiah's reform, just before the Exile, abolished these local shrines and concentrated all worship in the Temple of Jerusalem. After the Exile it was the synagogue which catered for the religious needs both of the country people and of the dispersed of Israel. The Pharisees performed a great service for the Jews by the creation of the synagogue, by their insistence on the duty of prayer, and by their conception of the future life and the Messianic kingdom. But their religion tended to become dry, formal and legalistic. Placing the strict observance of the Law in the forefront of religion they gradually supplemented and developed it by a vast oral tradition characterized by a punctilious attention to detail and a growing tendency to place legal purity above morality. In this way they became estranged from the masses.

One other party should be mentioned. Although less prominent than the others its influence was considerable, and we shall have more to say of it later on. This was the Essenes, who sought purity by isolation from the world and who dwelt apart in coenobitic communities, mostly around the Dead Sea. It has been suggested that they originated as ultra-strict Pharisees who found it impossible to carry out all the minute requirements of the laws of purity in ordinary life; but they soon developed some distinctive features of considerable interest which mark them off from the Pharisees.

Outside of all these parties was the great mass of ordinary people, the toiling, ignorant, simple-minded masses, the *Ebionim*—literally 'the poor in spirit'. For them a pilgrimage to the Temple at Jerusalem and participation in its worship was a luxury they could only on rare occasions afford. For the study of the Law they were too ignorant, and for the scrupulous observance of all the minute rules and complicated ceremonial obligations strained from it by the Scribes and Pharisees they had neither the time nor the leisure, occupied as they were in nearly all their waking hours with earning their daily bread. Therefore they were despised and ostracized by the practitioners of legal righteousness, regarded as mere sinners and classed with the publicans and the heathen. To these Ebionim it seemed that religion was something from which they were shut out just because they were poor and ignorant and had to work so hard for their living. Yet they nourished the hope that evil could not always be triumphant, that somehow God would intervene and justify the good, with whom they tended to identify the poor and the humble. To this class the political oppression of the Jewish nation was merely one symptom of the universal triumph of wickedness which was enthroned the whole world over. The world had grown so evil that God must surely intervene and 'put down the mighty from their seats and exalt the humble and meek, fill the hungry with good things and send the rich empty away.'

It was in this atmosphere that the apocalyptic literature grew up and it was to this spiritually destitute mass that it made its appeal. It provided a popular and acceptable solution to the problems which obsessed them. Now that the Law had assumed a position of finality as a result of the work of the Scribes there was no further place for its supplementation by prophecy. Therefore the prophetic visionaries who produced the apocalyptic literature ascribed their revelations to the great seers of antiquity. Of these the most popular was Enoch, and in the first century BC a whole literature ascribed to him was produced which enjoyed extraordinary popularity and coloured the thoughts and beliefs of every pious Jew. It was regarded by the masses as Scripture and the first Book of Enoch is quoted as such in the New Testament Epistle of Jude.

Characteristic of apocalyptic literature is a highly developed angelology and demonology derived from Persian religion with its conception of the eternal struggle between Ahura-Mazda and Ahriman, the forces of Light and the forces of Darkness. The origin of evil in the world is attributed to the unholy union of angels and women as recorded in the sixth chapter of Genesis, 'when the sons of God came in unto the daughters of men and they bare children unto them'. After the earth had been cleansed by the Flood these wicked angels and their half-human offspring became demons of the air, hovering over the earth 'seeking rest and finding none' unless they could take possession of some human or animal body. They are permitted to work their will until the final judgement, when they will be chained or burned in fire. This is the conception of evil spirits which is assumed throughout the Synoptic Gospels.

A second characteristic is the idea of the Day of Judgement which will end the present age and inaugurate 'the Age to Come'. The wicked, both angels and men, will be cast into outer darkness or burned in fire, the earth will be cleansed and the righteous, 'the faithful remnant', the true Israel will live in a regenerated world, 'the kingdom of the saints'. This Life of the Age to Come is not conceived as spiritual life in a heavenly sphere but as bodily life on a regenerated earth.

Thirdly, this Kingdom of the Saints will be ruled by the Messiah, who will also preside at the Day of Judgement. He will establish a New Jerusalem, the dispersed of Israel will be gathered in, and the Gentiles will be converted and subject to him. In the Book of Enoch this coming Messianic ruler is identified with that 'Son of Man' chosen before the world was created and he will be revealed from Heaven in a supernatural manner when the 'End of the Age' shall come.[1]

It is impossible to appreciate the significance attached by contemporaries to the coming of Jesus otherwise than against this background. The Synoptic presentation of his message and teaching is saturated through and through with apocalyptic ideas and language. The whole apocalyptic cosmology and eschatology, with its distinctive views on the source of evil, the nature of the demons, the final judgement, and the condemnation of the wicked with the appearance of the Son of Man in the clouds, are constantly presupposed. A high proportion of the most characteristic passages in the Synoptic Gospels are from the apocalyptic literature and particularly from I Enoch. As R. H. Charles, the translator of the book of Enoch, observed: 'It is impossible to see Matthew, Mark and Luke in true perspective unless we place them against the background of the Book of Enoch.'

It is perfectly evident that the Apostles themselves were so dominated by the ideas of their race and period that they utterly failed to comprehend the real significance which Jesus intended his Passion to have. Even the tremendous experiences which convinced them of his resurrection and transformed them from a despondent and not outstandingly courageous group of men into a band of zealous and intrepid missionaries did nothing whatever to change their eschatological views. Though their fear and sorrow had been changed to joy and hope it was still popular apocalypse which coloured all their thoughts and conditioned all their reasoning. If they had beforehand been at a loss to understand when Jesus spoke of his death, they were as far as ever from comprehending it now, and the very last words they are recorded as addressing to him were, 'Lord, dost thou at this time restore again the kingdom of Israel?' (Acts 1: 6).

Jesus was the Christ; of that they were convinced. But they were still Jews of their period and Christ was conceivable to them only in the accepted framework of prophecy and apocalypse. How was this framework to be reconciled with his suffering, death, and resurrection? They remembered that he had foretold his Passion and had applied the suffering servant prophecies to himself. Therefore it seemed to them that he could only have meant that the Messiah had necessarily to fulfil all these prophecies about himself first, and *then* he would return in glory: 'Ought not Christ to have suffered these things and enter into his glory?' (Luke 24: 26). Incomprehensible and outrageous as it had seemed at first that the Messiah should suffer and be rejected, they were forced by their experiences to the conclusion that all that he had undergone formed a part of these prophecies. Everything that had happened had occurred 'in order that the Scriptures might be fulfilled'. The rejection, suffering, and death of Jesus were therefore the pre-ordained living proof of his Messiahship and, since the prophecies had thus far been fulfilled, the time left for repentance before his return in glory to judge the world must be short. This is the whole tenor of Peter's first speeches and the whole atmosphere of the Apostolic Church as described in the Acts of the Apostles: 'Him being delivered by the determinate counsel and foreknowledge of God . . . Therefore let all the house of Israel know assuredly that God hath made that same Jesus, whom ye have crucified, both Lord and Christ' (Acts 2: 23–36).

Wherever Christianity was presented to persons of Jewish faith the arguments for it had always to be from the prophecies of Scripture, and always the one incomprehensible feature to all Jews was the suffering of the Messiah. 'Paul, as his manner was . . . reasoned with them out of the Scriptures, opening and alleging that Christ must needs have suffered and risen again from the dead; and that this Jesus, whom I preach unto you, is Christ' (Acts 17: 3). The message, as presented by the first Apostles, is still the coming of the man from Heaven to judge the world: 'He hath appointed a day, in the which he will judge the world in righteousness by that man whom he hath ordained' (Acts 17: 31).

This preaching that Jesus was the promised Messiah and that he had died and risen again met with bitter opposition wherever it was preached to orthodox Jews. Time and again in the Acts of the Apostles it is the Jews who stir up opposition against this 'sect of the Nazarenes' while in those early days there is no hint of opposition or hostility to the preaching of Christianity from non-Jews. The earliest persecutions of the Church, the martyrdom of Stephen and of James, the imprisonment of Peter, and all the opposition created to the teaching of Paul, leading to his imprisonment, came exclusively from the Jews. The civil authorities of the Roman Empire showed themselves not only tolerant but, on several occasions, actively intervened to save Paul from the hostility of the Jews. The explanation of this is not that God had hardened their hearts and rejected His chosen people in order to give the vineyard to others, so that the Scriptures may be fulfilled, as contemporaries naively supposed. It was simply because, to the Jews, the idea of a divine being who dies and rises again was incomprehensible and blasphemous. Therefore, by sheer force of circumstances, the Gospel came to be preached more and more to the Gentiles. Among them, not only did it in many places receive a tolerant hearing, it was often eagerly welcomed, for in the Hellenistic world of that period to die and rise again was exactly what a divine being was expected to do. In the atmosphere of that period the death of Jesus could only be satisfactorily explained in terms of Hellenistic thought. The reconciling synthesis is the achievement of St Paul, by birth a Jew, by training a Pharisee, but born in a Hellenistic university town and deeply influenced by the Hellenized Judaism of the Wisdom literature. Through him the Apostolic Church came to terms with the prevailing setting of Hellenistic salvation religions and became sacramental.

This transference of the Gospel from Jewish to Gentile soil was the outstanding fact in the early history of the Church. To understand this, however, it is necessary to go a very long way back.

11

The Gentile Setting

THE religious experience of primitive peasant societies was conditioned by their close contact with the mysteries of life and growth and by their dependence upon the rhythm of the seasons and the fertility of the soil. Whereas pastoral and hunting peoples thought of the divine powers as formidable and incalculable, to be propitiated or obeyed, the peasant peoples conceived the numinous as a dependable life-giving power which men could learn to co-operate with and even control by the performance of the appropriate rituals. Out of this experience grew the conception of the Great Mother, the source of life, and of her fertilizing consort, the dying and reviving vegetation god. When, as frequently happened, pastoral peoples overran agricultural communities, the old vegetation gods were considered as having been overcome by the sky gods, just as the peoples were subjected to their new warrior overlords. From the fusion of cultures which resulted, new syncretistic pantheons were developed in which the old gods tended to be relegated to the underworld, where they ruled over the dead, while the sky gods reigned in Heaven over the living. Later on, when great military monarchies arose, they developed an imposing state religion with a powerful priesthood celebrating a sun god of whom the monarch with his glittering court was an image. But if the new sun gods became supreme in the state religions, the old vegetation gods retained the popular affections, the more so as the all-powerful military and imperial state with its court and priesthood was remote from the ordinary life of the people in a way that the former agricultural state religions had not been. This had important consequences because the old popular religions thereby changed their function. Now that their observance was no longer indispensable to the maintenance of society, this function being taken over by the state religion, they became personal religions for the individual. They also became other-worldly and spiritualized, and finally acquired an ethical and moral significance as their prehistoric crudity was gradually refined away. The great upheavals and conquests of the first millenium BC had a most important influence on this process. This was a time when ambitious conquerors aspired to found universal empires, great armies marched and fought, pillaged and slew. The Assyrian, Chaldaean and Persian Empires in turn rose and fell, followed by Alexander the Great and then the Romans. The submergence of the old states and the obliteration of their boundaries led to the discrediting of the earlier conceptions of local and national gods who were unable to provide any safeguard. It was above all the great state religions which were totally discredited, for their power was bound up with that of the state and could not survive its subjection. As a result of these conditions of disillusion, bewilderment, and sense of spiritual insecurity, the worship of the older vegetation gods, now transformed into private religions of personal salvation, re-emerged with a new significance.

The characteristic feature of the vegetation god is his triumph over death. He was conceived of as ruling in the spirit world. At first only the king was identified with him at death, but gradually others were accorded this privilege if they were considered worthy and acceptable to the god. There thus developed two conceptions of far-reaching importance to religion: the idea of a future life after death, and the idea that to acquire this immortality a man must show himself worthy of it and be acceptable to the god who confers it.

The conquest of the ancient world by Alexander the Great had a more permanent and far-reaching effect than previous conquests in that it brought about the cultural unification of that world and imparted to everything a Hellenic colouring. The Greek language, Greek thought, philosophy and culture penetrated everywhere and provided a unifying factor. All the old national and traditional forms, ways of thought, philosophies and religious systems were reinterpreted in terms of Greek ideas and often re-presented in a Greek dress. And to this new cultural unity of the ancient world, Rome added political unity.

We have seen that the old national religious cults were being transformed under the pressure of circumstances into personal religions. As such, and when re-presented in Greek dress to a world which was once more being united under the aegis of a common Hellenistic culture and civilization, their fundamental similarities become apparent. At the same time the mixing of populations and the disappearance of the old local loyalties led to a religious eclecticism in which the terminology and distinctive conceptions of these new personal religions were freely interchanged. This process was frequently aided by the deliberate policy of the new Greek rulers, and the old faiths were reinterpreted and spiritualized along the same lines as had already been adopted in Greece.

In the heroic period of the Homeric poems the old nature deities are in the background and the most prominent place is given to the Olympian sky gods. But, as in Egypt and elsewhere, it was the old gods who retained the popular affections and in the sixth century BC they re-emerged transformed by spiritual and other-worldly conceptions.

The followers of Orpheus, a semi-mythical character who may be historical, refined and transformed the old crude ecstatic nature worship of Dionysus into a ritual of purification. The old legends were reinterpreted in a spiritual sense and revealed as allegories in which the gods themselves had taught the truth of their being to men and shown them the way to acquire immortality and communion with them. The Orphic schools developed and gave prominence to ideas of which there is no trace in the Homeric religion, but which became fundamental to the new Mystery Religions: the conception of sin, and the need for atonement and purification, the suffering and death of a divine man, and the promise through him to his followers of a blessed immortality and liberation from the bondage of matter and the wheel of birth and death. From the crude orgiastic nature worship of the masses Orphism drew off an élite whose spiritual aspirations could not be satisfied by the old forms, and these grouped themselves in exclusive esoteric brotherhoods in which stress was laid on a life of abstinence, asceticism, and moral endeavour by which they should attain to the privilege of an ecstatic union with the divine, no longer as a delirious subconscious experience but as super-conscious spiritual communion.

The mystery schools were the characteristic expression of the Greek religious genius. Wherever Hellenic culture penetrated it encountered ancient vegetation rites that showed close affinities to those of Greece. These were reinterpreted and spiritualized in the same way as the Orphic schools and the Eleusinian mysteries had spiritualized the old popular legends of Greece. For example, in Egypt the Greek king Ptolemy Soter brought in one of the Eumolpid family from Eleusis to reform the Osiris worship and make of it a new Egypto-Hellenic mystery religion which should serve as a means of drawing together his Greek and Egyptian subjects. The Egyptian religion had at this time sunk into decadence and was disfigured by popular fetishism, animal-worship, and crude superstition. Here again there was an élite which sought a more spiritual interpretation of the old legends while still clinging to their national religious traditions. The basic resemblances made syncretism easy. Even before the time of Herodotus, Osiris had been identified with Dionysus and Isis with Demeter. Isis, whose most popular representation now was as the divine Mother suckling the infant Horus, was identified with the queen of heaven in all her forms, as Selene, as Hera, as Juno. She became the patroness of sailors and merchants who spread her worship to every part of the Roman Empire, and in Rome itself in the first century AD the Egyptian mysteries provided the first example of a popular personal religion triumphing over the resistance of the civil authorities and the official clergy.

Similar developments took place all over the Hellenistic world, either spontaneously or with official encouragement. Common to all the cults which developed was the idea of a supernatural being who had found the way to happiness and immortality, generally after suffering and a brutal death at the hands of evil forces. He now reigned in a spiritual realm and was able to confer on his followers the secret, the 'mystery' of how this deification could be accomplished. They too could follow his path, become united with him and share in his blessedness, provided they were pure and worthy. The ceremonies, 'the Mysteries', of the cult were designed to enable these followers to repeat the experience of their founder and share his triumph. The central idea of all of them was the promise of salvation or redemption, a deliverance from the bondage of fate or of evil forces by means of rebirth or regeneration. This regeneration was to be obtained through mystical association with the death and resurrection of a divine man, who himself was originally associated with vegetation. It was from this association that the idea of rebirth had in fact arisen.

The Greek philosophers meanwhile, particularly the Stoics and the Platonists, were conceiving the universe as a vast organism animated by the divine. Man was a microcosm, a universe in miniature, and his soul a spark of the cosmic fire. The elements were conceived as divine forces or cosmic energies acting under pre-determined law, the Divine *Pronoia* or Providence. The deities of the earlier civilizations which had succumbed to Hellenistic culture were allegorized as cosmic forces or as personified aspects of the supreme divinity. The way was thus opened to an abstract philosophical monotheism, and also to the theory of a hierarchy of eons or emanations between the Absolute and the Manifold, which played a great part in Gnostic speculations. This philosophy found itself in close harmony with the theology of the Chaldeans and the two influenced each other mutually. In the first century BC the Syrian Stoic philosopher Posidonius produced an eclectic philosophy combining Pythagoras, Plato, Stoicism, and Chaldean sidereal theology which had a profound influence on the foremost thinkers of the time.

The effect of this climate of opinion upon the religious feeling of the time naturally varied according to the education, temperament, and immediate background of the individual. Upon the educated and aristocratic Roman with his deep sense of duty and *pietas*, it produced the ethical Stoicism of Seneca, Epictetus, and Marcus Aurelius. Since the whole movement of the cosmos is the fulfilment of divine law, evil is the attempt to assert one's own will against it. We live under an immutable destiny, therefore prayer and supplication is mere weakness; the duty of man lies in submission and resignation. Virtue consists in bearing one's fate with fortitude, and in this man has an opportunity for displaying a nobility of soul which is perhaps denied to the gods.

The majority could never accept a creed so austere and impersonal. The planets and the elements, the archons and world-rulers, were for them still personal, still sentient beings. As such they had feelings, were animated by something resembling human passions and sentiments. If they were good they could not be utterly unrelenting, utterly indifferent to the aspiration and worship of the human heart. They must be amenable to prayer and sacrifice. Or if, as the increasing influence of Persian dualist thought was beginning to suggest, they were evil powers, hostile to Man, then it must be possible to find some means of escaping from bondage to them by entering into relationship with the higher powers beyond and above them. This was the promise which the Mystery Religions held out, the promise of deliverance, 'salvation', which was to be obtained by mystical fellowship with a divine man who had found the way through suffering and death to a spiritual realm beyond the power of the 'world rulers of this darkness' (Ephesians 6: 12). Those of his followers who were worthy might share his experience and participate in his triumph. By 'initiation' into the Mysteries instituted by him a man would be 'saved', delivered from his bondage to Fate and thereby released from the fetters which bind ordinary human existence. He would pass from the condition of being a lost soul 'having no hope and without God in the world' (Ephesians 2:12), which lies under the dominion of evil powers or of immutable cosmic forces, into a state of renewal and rebirth—a condition of privilege, enlightenment, hope, in which 'Neither death nor life, neither angels nor principalities [*Archai*], neither the present nor the future, no powers of the Height or of the Depth, nor anything else in all creation, will be able to part us from God's love' (Romans 8: 38). He was freed also from the common mortal lot of death and assured of a glorious immortality, made 'meet to be [a partaker] of the inheritance of the saints in light, delivered from the power of darkness . . . And you being dead . . . hath he quickened together with him . . . blotting out the handwriting of ordinances that was against us' (Coloss. 2: 13–14).

The various Mystery cults differed in detail but they all taught that the supreme good is to be realized not in this world but in a life hereafter. There were three characteristic features in greater or lesser degrees common to all of them. The first was the idea of rebirth or

117

regeneration. The initiate was born anew. He died to the old man, and 'put on the new which is renewed after the image of Him' (Coloss. 3: 10). Often this was marked by the assumption of a new name and the rebirth was in some senses astrological. If the stars at birth had been unfavourable, then it was possible to contract out of this adverse fate by being 'born again' under more favourable auspices. More often, however, it was a moral rebirth. Sometimes, as in the Egyptian Mysteries, the initiate underwent a symbolic death and transformation. Sometimes it was a mystical or sacramental participation in the death and resurrection of the redeemer. The initiate was 'buried with him in baptism, wherein also ye are risen with him' (Coloss. 2: 12).

The use of sacraments was a second characteristic feature of the Mystery Religions. The ceremonies of the cult were symbolic acts of magical and miraculous potency instituted by the founder as a means of enabling his followers to repeat his own experiences, and thus to become identified with him and share his triumph. The two commonest forms of sacrament were rites of purification and a mystical meal. Purification was designed to purge away the taint of common mortality, 'to put off the old man which is of the earth, earthy, and put on the new man' (1 Cor. 15: 47–9; Eph. 4: 22–4). This purification frequently took the form of a symbolic washing in which the impurities of the old self were washed away, as in the lustrations at Eleusis and the sprinkling (Asperges) in the Egyptian Mysteries. Sometimes this washing was conceived as having such magical power that its efficacy was mechanical and could be performed even for the dead (cf. 1 Cor. 15: 29). More often, however, and in addition to washing, it was conceived as a moral purification. The body had to be purified by ascetic preparation, by prayer and fasting, so that the soul could be released for illumination, from which stage the initiate went on to *Epopteia*, full contemplation. These three stages of Purification, Illumination, and Epopteia were more or less universally recognized in all the Mystery Religions.

The mystical meal was reserved for the initiates who had passed through the stage of purification. It was sometimes thought of simply as a rite of fellowship, a common meal in which the god acted as host to his guests; but more often it was seen as a symbolic or mystical partaking of the god himself or a symbol of him.

The third characteristic feature was the revelation of the *Gnosis soterias*, the knowledge of salvation. This was a higher divine knowledge, concealed even from the Archons and world-rulers, the hidden wisdom of the Most High, 'the Mystery which hath been hid ... but is now made manifest to his saints' (Coloss. 1: 26). This higher knowledge was sometimes revealed by the use of symbols which communicated nothing directly to the intellect but the contemplation of which would open the way for the illuminati to direct mystical experience, as in the symbolic drama performed at Eleusis. Sometimes, as in the Orphic Mysteries, it was the actual communication of a secret doctrine, of esoteric knowledge.

All these various conceptions tended to overlap and be combined. The Mysteries had become completely denationalized; they were personal religions for the individual and transcended the boundaries of nation and status. All initiates were brothers no matter whence they came. ('There is neither Greek nor Jew, barbarian nor Scythian, bond nor free' [Coloss. 3: 11].) The quest for salvation was universal and some men went from one Mystery school to another, inevitably carrying with them the distinctive conceptions of one school and blending and reinterpreting them in terms of another.

In this atmosphere Christianity too was regarded as a Mystery Religion. Indeed the preceeding paragraphs show that the letters of St Paul are full of the characteristic conceptions of this Hellenistic climate of opinion. This was inevitable. 'The new faith poured its revelation into the hallowed moulds of earlier religions because in that form alone could the world in which it developed receive its message.' (Cumont, *Oriental Religions in Roman Paganism.*) Given this background, this psychological climate, in what other way could a religion whose starting point was the death and resurrection of a divine man, a pre-ordained king, be interpreted? The death of the Messiah, so incomprehensible to the Jews, at once made sense to the Greeks, sense of the sublimest and most truly religious kind they could imagine. As Dean Inge says in his essay on St Paul:

It was as a Mystery Religion that Europe accepted Christianity. Just as the Jewish Christians took with them the whole framework of Apocalyptic Messianism, and set the figure of Jesus within it, so the Greeks took with them the whole scheme of the Mysteries, with their sacraments, their purifications and fasts, their idea of a mystical brotherhood, and their doctrine of 'salvation' (Soteria is essentially a mystery word) through membership in a divine society, worshipping Christ as the patronal deity of their mysteries. Historically this type of Christianity was the origin of Catholicism, both Western and Eastern.

But also, given these conditions, Christianity was bound to triumph, for not only could it offer all that the Mysteries had to give but immense advantages in addition.

In the first place the Mystery Schools were very exclusive. Only an élite could secure admission to their privileges. But everyone longed for salvation: 'redemption from servitude . . . was the object of the intensest craving in the higher life of pagan society' (H. A. Kennedy in *St Paul and the Mystery Religions*), and this was offered freely by the Apostles. All could participate in the blessed immortality conferred by

Jesus, the Mysteries were thrown open to everyone regardless of his past, his ignorance or his sins. All that was necessary for salvation was to believe in Jesus Christ and to confess him Lord.

Secondly, Jesus was no shadowy myth but a real historical person. Among those who preached him were many who had actually seen him in the flesh, or at least knew of those who had. A great weakness of the Mystery Religions lay in the crudity of the barbarous legends of the primitive stages of belief from which they had emerged and which philosophy and allegory could not wholly eradicate. But the background to Christianity was the ethical monotheism of the Jews; and this too was a factor of great importance. The philosophical speculation of the period was tending more and more strongly towards monotheism. But the Mystery cults were many and various, 'gods many and lords many', whereas Christianity proclaimed 'There is one God and one Lord' (1 Cor. 8: 5–6). Some reconciling synthesis was bound to emerge ultimately from the chaos of philosophies and cults in the early Roman Empire and religious unity was bound to follow political unity. For the mass of mankind certainty is a primary requisite of religion. If he cannot find that certainty within himself as the fruit of his own experience he cannot remain satisfied with a suspension of belief, a philosophic doubt. The simultaneous presentation of a dozen conflicting revelations of the one truth is an intolerable situation. The average man demands of a revealed religion that it produce an acceplable title to say with divine authority that it is true; and if true, then everything else must be false. Christianity, as the heir of Jewish exclusive monotheism, proclaimed itself from the first as the one true religion and steadfastly refused compromise or alliance with any other cult. All the other rites were the inventions of the demonic powers, the other gods were classed with the Archons and world-rulers who are coming to nought, and their resemblances to Christian rites were explained, in the ingenious sophistry of Justin Martyr, as the demons' attempts to 'plagiarise Christianity by anticipation'. The Old Testament was here a powerful ally. The prophetic denunciations of the Baalim, whose worship was so often set up against that of Jehovah, were applied to the cults of other gods. In the declining years of the Roman Empire this was a religion which made far more appeal to the degenerate and discouraged masses, avid for certainty in the next world if they had no security in this, than the easy tolerance of the last pagan philosophers.

But if Christianity steadfastly refused to compromise on the uniqueness of the God it proclaimed, this by no means prevented converts from bringing with them the religious conceptions with which they were already familiar and continuing many of the modes of worship to which they were accustomed, after reinterpreting them in a

Christian sense. 'The essence of paganism implies that the nature of a divinity broadens as the number of its votaries increases—everyone credits it with some new quality and its character becomes more complex' (Cumont, *op. cit.*) This tendency, inevitable in any case, was officially encouraged by the Church, particularly after the conversion of Constantine when the masses poured into the Church. Of the religions of the later Roman Empire which in this way profoundly influenced Christianity, three were of particular importance.

From the first century AD the Egyptian Mysteries of Isis and Serapis had become universally popular, especially in Southern Italy where the favourite image of Isis was that of the Divine Mother and Child. King in his book *The Gnostics and their Remains* shows how the popular Isis worship of this period is in every detail the forerunner of the Catholic cult of the Madonna. Her form, her symbols, her distinctive rites, came straight into Christianity. The priests of Isis wore the tonsure and were vowed to celibacy, the sistrum became the bell, and the lotus borne by her votaries, the lily. A sard of this period even depicts Isis with the inscription 'Immaculate is Our Lady Isis'. The ceremony of sprinkling the worshippers for purification before the celebration of the Mysteries has become the Asperges ceremony, while the mitre and crozier of Christian bishops are thought to derive their origin from the high crown and crook of the Egyptian gods.

In the days of Imperial Rome the old traditional religion of the city state lost all vitality and withered away. Though its rites and festivals were still observed by force of custom and the prestige of long usage, and still had official status, as a religion it had long ceased to have any real meaning or influence. It had never transformed itself by means of philosophical allegory and mystical symbolism into a personal religion as other national cults had done. Consequently it had become 'a thing devoid of sense whose raison d'être was no longer understood; it embodied dead ideas and an obsolete conception of the world' (Cumont). As the state religion for a world-wide imperial monarchy it was a hopeless anachronism.

The Emperor Aurelian therefore determined to substitute for it a religion more in tune with the spirit of the age and the growing demand for monotheism. As the official religion of the Empire he adopted the solar monotheism which had been evolved in Syria out of the fusion of Chaldean astrology with the Stoic mystical philosophy of Posidonius, and which had long been popular in Rome. Sol Invictus, the Invincible Sun, was a symbol perfectly adapted to the requirements of the military dictator of a world-wide empire, and it remained the imperial emblem of the One God even after Constantine the Great had adopted Christianity, as is shown by numerous coins and inscriptions of the fourth century. Constantine and his sons quite evidently saw nothing in it incompatible with Christianity, nor, it may safely be assumed, did the majority of their subjects. We know that the Christology of the first Christian emperors always tended to be Arian. They were soldiers and practical statesmen for whom the Sun was a far more fitting symbol of the One God than a Jewish tribal deity, and who could far more easily conceive of Christ as the subordinate son of the Almighty Father than understand the metaphysical subtleties of the Athanasian Trinity.

The official celebration of the birthday of the Invincible Sun on 25 December was adopted first at Rome as the birthday of Christ (it was also the birthday of Mithra) and thence passed to all the Christian world. St John Chrysostom, Patriarch of Constantinople, writing in 385 says, 'It is not ten years since this day was first known to us'.

Of all the pagan religions which flourished in the last days of the Roman Empire none, apart perhaps from Christianity, was so popular as Mithraism. It can be briefly described as a form of Zoroastrianism greatly simplified and adapted to the West. While Persian dualism was a fundamental feature of it, Mithraism derived only its mythology and ritual from Persia. In all other respects its theology was entirely Chaldean and did not notably differ from the solar monotheism of Syria. It was therefore perfectly compatible with the official worship of Sol Invictus and functioned in practice in close alliance with it.

The distinctive feature of Mithraism was the Mazdean conception of the Universe as the scene of the constant struggle for mastery between the forces of Light, created by Ahura-Mazda the divine principle of good, and the forces of Darkness, created by his adversary Ahriman, the eternal principle of evil and adversary of good. In consequence, Mithraism was a virile creed, making a great appeal to soldiers, and was carried by them to every part of the Empire. In contrast to the religions of contemplative mysticism or sensous ceremonial, Mithraism was a creed of action and freely employed military metaphors. Life is a combat, a constant battle against evil. The believer is enrolled as a soldier of Mithra in his army of saints to fight for him in his holy war against the hosts of the devil. Christian military symbolism and metaphor, the idea of the Church Militant and Christian soldiers who 'fight the good fight', for example, undoubtedly owe their origin to Mithraic influence.

Mithraism also had its sacramental side. Besides the initiation of the Taurobolium, the dreadful baptism in blood, there was a sacramental meal of bread and wine eaten in commemoration of the last supper which Mithra was said to have eaten with his companions before his ascension to Heaven. The bread at this supper was in the form of a round flat cake, symbolizing the solar disk, and called Mizd. King (*op.*

cit.) considers that this was the prototype of the Host and that the word Mass (Missa) is derived from Mizd, since the popular derivation from the words 'Ite, missa est' is absurd.

Although this account gives but the barest summary of Mithraism, enough has been said to show how closely it resembled Christianity. That it borrowed many features from Christianity cannot be doubted, and it will always be a matter of dispute among scholars to determine in many cases which religion is the originator and which the borrower. Mithra's last supper with his companions before ascending to heaven would seem almost certainly to be a plagiarism of Christianity; as is the legend of shepherds coming to his birth, for this story makes nonsense of the context of the legend in which it occurs. On the other hand, King (in *The Gnostics and their Remains*) shows that the story of the three Magi is in all probability derived from Mithraism. The important point for our purpose is that at the decisive period when the long evolution of the climate of opinion was moving irresistibly towards the institutionalizing of a universal (catholic) religion of syncretistic monotheism, Mithraism, in partnership with Sol Invictus, and Christianity had become in effect the only possible candidates. 'If Christianity had been checked in its growth by some deadly disease the world would have become Mithraic,' said Ernest Renan (quoted by Cumont). As it was, in the early fourth century, the final choice between the two must have seemed to hang by a thread, and the imperial favour veered from one to the other with disconcerting rapidity. Only a few years after Diocletian had made a determined effort to extirpate Christianity altogether, it became under Constantine the religion of the imperial court. Civil wars and disputed successions added to the confusion and uncertainty. While Constantine reigned in Gaul, Spain, and Britain, the three emperors who between them ruled the rest of the Roman world met at Carnuntum on the Danube and there solemnly dedicated an altar to Mithra as 'the protector of the Empire' (AD 307). Six years later came the Edict of Milan, but who could then foresee that it would not be reversed by another revolution within a few years? The bewildered populace found adherence to Christianity persecuted at one moment and at the next an avenue to favour and advancement. What more natural than that in times of persecution Christians continued to worship Christ under Mithraic symbols, and when the tables were turned in the next revolution Mithraists continued to worship Mithra under Christian symbols? In this way the confusion of rites, symbolism and legends has become inextricable; but becuase Christianity became official, the names and the outward colouring were bound to be Christian. While the popular local deities of rural paganism became Christian saints and Isis became the Virgin Mother, Mithra, now identified with Michael, captain of the Heavenly Host, still waged his holy war against Ahriman, now renamed Satan.

For the ignorant masses Christianity and Mithraism were to all intents and purposes identical. At that period these masses were as sheeplike and subservient to authority as the subjects of any totalitarian state. It has been estimated that at the accession of Constantine the number of genuine Christians in the Empire was between 5 and 10 per cent of the total population. But when they became the dominant party in the state the masses hastened to conform to the established ideology; and it is the masses who determine the outward and popular forms of religion.

The Protestant Reformation was largely a reaction against these popular outward forms imported into Christianity by its pagan adherents and institutionalized by the Roman Church. It aimed to strip off pagan accretions and return to what was distinctive of Christianity. This meant in practice the Holy Scriptures and the Pauline theology. But these also are the product of accretion, compromise, and development. To appreciate this we must now go back and trace the stages by which the Gospel was transformed in the course of its proclamation.

12

The Evolution of Catholic Christianity and The Making of the New Testament

WE HAVE now seen that Christianity was first proclaimed in the setting of Jewish Apocalypse. Christ was regarded as having fulfilled the Messianic prophecies and 'by his obedience even unto death' had been exalted to the right hand of God, whence at the appointed time, He will return in glory as the promised Son of Man to judge the world. On the other hand, when the Gospel was proclaimed in the setting of the Greek Mystery Religions, Christ came to be regarded as a reedemer god who by his death rescued man from thraldom to the powers of darkness and made him to be a partaker of His immortality. These two conceptions, apparantly so contradictory, were largely synthesized by the genius of St Paul. His Pharisaic theory of Atonement here played an indispensible part, for it was this alone which could provide a bridge of reconciliation between the Jewish and the Gentile conceptions of what Christ's redemption meant. Out of this synthesis, with sundry accretions from other prevailing modes of religious thought, grew that Catholic Christianity which ultimately secured universal acceptance as the one and only 'Apostolic' Christianity.

But in the first century there was no such thing as a universally recognized body of Christian teaching. Every Church had its own distinctive presentation. In the first two generations after the Crucifixion there was an extraordinarily rapid and wide diffusion of the Christian message. The kernel of this message was that Jesus was a divine being who had been crucified and had risen again from the dead. But upon this basis every conceivable kind of interpretation was placed by those who heard it. Christianity was one thing in Jerusalem. It was quite another in Antioch, and yet another in Ephesus, in Corinth, in Alexandria, in Rome. For the first ten years or so after the Crucifixion Jerusalem was the headquarters of Christianity and it remained purely Jewish. But gradually Antioch became the most active centre, and remained so for at least a generation. Here the doctrinal setting and background is still the Old Testament, but the Jewish Law is no longer binding; Christ has supplemented it by a new covenant.

At Antioch, Christianity is still Judaeo-Hellenic. But towards the end of the first century Ephesus becomes the most active centre of Christianity. Here the Gospel is proclaimed in an atmosphere of Hellenized orientalism and sacramental mysticism. The emphasis shifts from the Crucifixion to the Incarnation, from the Messianic king to the Cosmic Logos, from the historical prophet 'mighty in word and deed' to the indwelling Christ. Towards the end of the second century the centre shifts to Rome, and with it there is a reaction to authority, the development of institutionalism, organization, definition, discipline, together with a great development of outward forms and rites.

Catholic Christianity did not therefore spring full grown from the divine mission in Palestine like Athene from the head of Zeus. It was a product of gradual growth, of compromise, synthesis and development from the clash and interplay of conflicting views. It was not one, comprehensive, 'true' version of Christianity which existed from the outset and emerged triumphant after a struggle against heresies and false teaching. In fact the Catholic Church cannot be said to exist before the latter part of the second century—and neither can the New Testament. They both grew together out of the need for standardization which the rapid growth and wide dissemination of the Gospel message made imperative. The canon of the New Testament is both the product and the monument of that search for a *via media,* and it bears all the marks of its origin. When Protestantism went back to the New Testament in search of the 'faith once and for all delivered to the saints' it was going back simply to another product of accretion and development. The New Testament itself was the outcome of that clash of traditions and settings in which the first Christians sought to understand the Christian revelation.

From one point of view the story of the development of Christianity is the story of its gradual emancipation from Judaism. But this was an emanicipation from Jewish practice much more than from doctrine. Paul's great revolt was from Jewish legalism and ceremonial obligation but his theology and his conception of the divine remained to the end predominantly Rabbinic. During the thirty years of his ministry he carried the Gospel a long way from its original setting, and by the end of his life he was preaching something radically different from the Apostolic Christianity with which he had begun. Nevertheless, right to the end, despite all his concessions to the Hellenistic setting in which he preached, and the modifications and developments to which he was led by his own religious experience, he retained his essentially Jewish conception of the nature of God—as unique, as personal, as Creator of this world, and as all-good. Moreover, by his theory of Atonement, derived from his Pharisaic education, he succeeded in

126

reconciling this conception of God with the function which the Mystery Religion environment necessarily assigned to Christ.

It has been estimated that in the first century AD there were perhaps five million persons of Jewish faith in the Roman Empire. The great majority of these, however, were no more than semi-Jews. They were not Jews by birth, but 'proselytes' or 'resident strangers', as they are called in the Talmud and the Acts of the Apostles. Wherever there were pagans who lived in close contact with Jewish communities a considerable number found themselves attracted by the monotheism and high ethical code of the Jewish religion; but they were as a rule repelled by the obligation of circumcision and the rigid rules of ceremonial purity, so that very few of them became full converts or 'proselytes of righteousness' bound to assume the whole yolk of the Law. These therefore formed a fringe of half-Jews round the synagogues of the Dispersion and to this class Christianity offered exactly the religion they were seeking.

The earliest Christian congregations grew up alongside the synagogues and were modelled on them. Those who accepted Christ were already imbued with the Old Testament conception of God and to them the Pauline Gospel was particularly well adapted. It was in fact precisely the emancipation from Jewish practice while retaining the core of Jewish theology that they required. So long, therefore, as this class of persons remained the most important element in the Church there could be no question of discarding the Jewish doctrinal basis of Christianity, and there would be a vigorous reaction against any attempt to do so. This reaction necessarily took the form of an appeal to synagogue standards and the authority of 'Scriptures'.

In the meantime the Gospel was spreading more and more among persons who were quite unfamiliar with the Old Testament. In these circumstances its meaning changed still more, and by a logical development of the ideas already inherent in the Pauline message it gradually assumed forms completely hostile to its Jewish setting. There was at this time, particularly in Asia, a strong tendency towards a dualist view of the universe. We have seen, in discussing the Hellenistic setting, how widespread was the belief that the universe is ruled by forces hostile or indifferent to Man, and that deliverance from their power was to be obtained by the revelation of a Gnosis or higher knowledge. St Paul, in fact, as his letters quite clearly show, went a very long way towards sharing these ideas. But he always confined them strictly within an ultimately Hebraic conception of the divine nature and regarded the essence of Christ's mission as his atoning sacrifice, in virtue of which man is reconciled to God and restored to his true place in the scheme of things above the archons and world-rulers whom he can henceforth ignore, since they are essentially on a lower spiritual plane than man ('Know ye not that we shall judge the angels').

But wherever the Gospel was preached outside Jewish or semi-Jewish circles, to persons unconnected with the Hebrew background, the tendency was to see as the essence of Christ's mission the revelation of a higher knowledge by which man achieves liberation from the unseen powers which govern this world. Where there is no longer the background of Jewish national history and prophetic Scripture, the tendency was for the Gospel to become mystical and psychological, to be interpreted as a cosmic drama rather than as an historical event.

This climate of opinion, which had been influenced by the thought of India and Persia and which was particularly strong in Asia, gave rise to what is known as Gnosticism. Its underlying principle is the theory that evil arises from matter. According to this view, the material universe, being manifestly imperfect, cannot be the creation of a God who is all-wise and all-powerful. It is unnecessary here to go into details of all the varied and complex theories of Creation which characterized the different Gnostic systems. It is enough to say that man was postulated as essentially a spirit created by the High God but who, either as a result of his own sins or the malice of demons, had fallen or been corrupted and was now encased in the prison of the material body and exiled in the material universe. His object, therefore, is to find some way of escaping from the bondage of matter and recovering his original state of purity. To people with these views Christ's mission was also conceived as a redemption, but it was primarily a liberation from the bondage of this evil world and from the power of the 'prince of this world'.

Deliverance from the prison of the material world and thraldom to its archons (the *Stoicheia* of St Paul's Epistles—e.g. Gal. 4: 9) was to be achieved both by sacramental means and by the communication of esoteric knowledge, an inner teaching or gnosis, which was reserved for initiates in the mysteries. Man was saved, not from sin but from ignorance; redemption was a teaching delivered, not an expiation. It was the aim of the angelic world-rulers to keep man in ignorance of his heavenly origin and divine nature, so that he should never seek to escape from their power and return to his Father's house. Jesus therefore was an emissary of the Most High God who was sent to recall to man 'that imperial palace whence he came' and reveal to him the road of return to it. Such a return usually involved a rigorous asceticism, a complete mortifying of the 'filthy carnal envelope' in order to set free the pure spirit. The material world and all its works were to be rejected as the creation and snare of the devil.

Gnostic ideas had a very considerable influence on the formative period of Catholic Christianity and have left many traces in the New Testament:

Love not the world, neither the things that are in the world. If any man love the world, the love of the Father is not in him. For all that is in the world, the lust of the flesh, and the lust of the eyes, and the pride of life, is not of the Father, but is of the world. (1 John 2: 15–17.)

We know that we belong to God and that the whole world lies in the power of the Evil One. (ibid, 5: 19.)

This seems to breathe a very different spirit from the Jesus who bade his hearers look upon the love of God manifested in 'the lilies of the field robed more gloriously than Solomon and the fowls of the air whom your heavenly Father feedeth', (Matt. 6: 26–9).

But in spite of the profound colouring imparted to Christianity by the Gnostic climate, the nucleus of most Christian communities was formed of those who had a doctrinal background of Jewish theology. There were two inevitable consequences which followed logically from dualist premises with which a faith nurtured in Judaism could not come to terms.

In the first place the Gnostics found themselves obliged to reject the Old Testament. It was not enough to discard Jewish ceremonial practices and to contend that Christ had substituted a new legal code of righteousness for that of Moses while still retaining the Jewish theological framework. If Christ had abrogated the Old Law, then He had abrogated the whole of it and not merely a part. Moreover, if this world is evil and yet the God of the Old Testament is its Creator, He cannot be the Father of Jesus Christ but can only be the Prince of Darkness, 'the Prince of this world' who 'hath nothing in me' (John 14: 30) and who is now judged (ibid. 16: 11). The contrast between the ethic preached by Jesus and the morality ascribed to Jehovah in the Old Testament seemed to the Gnostics a completely convincing proof of this. It followed therefore that Christ's mission had been above all to destroy and supersede the religion of the Jews and all that it stood for. The Hebrew element in early Christianity was, however, far too strong to tolerate this, and the multiplicity of the Gnostic sects, together with the grotesque exaggerations of some of them, made it impossible for Gnostic Christianity to withstand the compact and disciplined strength which Catholicism developed in the second and third centuries.

The second consequence of the dualist view of the universe as applied to Christianity was that if all matter is the creation of an evil power and the human body is a prison in which Satan has bound a spark of pure spirit, then Christ could not have had a real physical body. He must have been an eon, a pure spirit from on high whose physical form was merely illusory. This theory—Docetism, as it was called—provided a very simple explanation of His Resurrection and Ascension, but it made the Crucifixion quite unreal and meaningless.

According to one Gnostic view, Satan, or Jehovah, having stirred up the Jews (*his* Chosen People) to crucify Jesus, had merely vented his fury against an impassive phantom. Another, and more subtle, Gnostic view drew a distinction between the man Jesus and the eon Christ; Christ descended upon Jesus in the form of a dove at his baptism, guided his ministry, and left him on the Cross at the moment when he cried, 'My God, my God, why hast thou forsaken me?'

Since for the Gnostics the essence of Christ's mission lay in his revelation and not in his atoning sacrifice, this denial of his real humanity was not felt to be an objection. On the contrary, by emphasizing his separation from this evil world it also emphasized his divine status. But to the majority, nurtured in Judaism, it seemed to destroy the one feature of Christianity which distinguished it from the Mystery cults and in virtue of which it claimed superiority to them. These docetic views of Christ are strongly combated in the Epistles of John, whose author, however, was himself strongly influenced by the Gnostic view of the universe. All the Johannine writings in fact illustrate admirably the situation prevailing in Asia Minor at the beginning of the second century.

In the forty years following the death of Paul there had been a rapid development of his gospel in circles far removed from the Jewish religious background, circles steeped in Phrygian mysticism and Asian dualism. In these conditions the original Apostolic message not only shed all its apocalyptic colouring; it was spiritualized out of all recognition from the crude proclamation of the early days. But this process went so far that the more traditionally minded began to feel in danger of losing the historic person of Jesus altogether. On the other hand, they themselves had evolved too far from the Palestinian standpoint to be satisfied with the presentation of Jesus in the Synoptic Gospels. They required a presentation of Him more in accord with the later developments of Pauline Christology: 'The Fourth Gospel, as its Prologue forewarns, is an application to the story of Jesus as tradition reported it of the Pauline incarnation doctrine formulated under the Stoic Logos theory' (B. W. Bacon, *Making of the New Testament*, p. 231).

On the other hand, there was no concession to Docetism. Paul had waged a great struggle to free the Christian message from its swaddling bands of rigid Judaism. Now the churches of his mission field were faced with the opposite extreme: how to preserve the historical foundation of their faith and save it from evaporating altogether in what they conceived to be mystical and theosophical perversions. Between Ebionism on the one hand and Gnosticism on the other, the need to find some standard had become overwhelming. And it was not only a definition of doctrine that was required; it was also necessary to standardize practice on account of the spiritualistic excesses to which 'prophecy' gave rise in church meetings.

As soon as the need for some standard in doctrine and practice had become imperative it was inevitable that there should be a reaction to the methods and principles of the synagogue. The result was the emergence and authority of an ecclesiastical hierarchy and the formulation of a 'canon' of authorized Christian 'Scripture', both of which laid claim to Apostolic authority and depended for their validity on that claim.

The most characteristic feature of Christian meetings in the earliest times was a strong sense of the constant presence and inspiration of the Holy Spirit. But it was difficult to control and liable to lead to aberrations and abuses (cf. 1 Cor. 12 and 14). The claim to exercise these gifts began to be looked upon as dangerous and eventually as heretical. As the sense of the presence and authority of the spirit weakens, so the authority of the letter and of Church organization and discipline increases. On the one hand, the rapid growth and wide dissemination of the Gospel, and on the other the multiplication of differing interpretations of it according to the background of those who received it, were making standardization imperative. This took two forms: first, the consolidation of Church organization, the insistence on obedience to bishops as the successors of the Apostles and heirs of their authority; and second, the appeal to Apostolic writings.

The custom of reading from the Scriptures at weekly meetings led naturally to a gradual supplementing of the Old Testament by specifically Christian writings. The first of these were no doubt 'Epistles' on the Pauline model. But there was also great scope for recorded visions and inspired messages of the spirit. The Shepherd of Hermas, for example, was one such work which enjoyed widespread popularity and was regarded as genuinely inspired Christian 'Scripture'. As time went on, however, it was felt that only works which could claim real Apostolic authorship should be admitted to the canon. The period of formulation of the New Testament canon is the second half of the second century. This was the time when Christianity was gradually condensing into the Catholic Church, rejecting its extremes, and finding a *via media* between Marcion and the Gnostics on the one hand, who repudiated the Old Testament and the Jewish setting of Christianity altogether, and, on the other, the Ebionites, who persisted in retaining the whole Hebrew framework. But it is not until the fourth century that the canon definitely became fixed at just the books it contains now. During the whole of this long formative period the text even of these was subject to continual revision and editing to pare away whatever concessions they might contain to what evolving orthodoxy was coming to regard as heretical.

The letters of Paul are the oldest part of the New Testament. It seems that at an early date these were collected into a corpus, but the first person known to have used such a collection and treated it as Scripture is the heretic Marcion. He was a native of Asia Minor who was very active in Rome in the middle of the second century. The churches which adhered to his doctrines were widespread and flourishing until the official establishment of Christianity by Constantine, when they were condemned as heretical and proscribed. They continued to flourish, however, to the east of the Roman Empire until the fifth century, and it was Marcionite Christianity which contributed the Christian element to Manichaeism.

Marcion wrote a book—now lost—called *Antitheses*, in which he placed side by side the references to God in the Old Testament, on one hand, and in the recorded words of Jesus and the Epistles of Paul on the other. These showed such striking contrasts that Marcion contended they could not possibly refer to the same deity. He therefore made a distinction between the 'Good God', the Father of Jesus Christ, and the 'Just God' of the Old Testament. He did not go so far as to assert that the latter was an evil power, but simply that he was inferior and, relative to the 'Good God', imperfect. Unlike other Gnostic teachers he does not seem to have made any attempt to evolve an elaborate speculative theological system to define the relation between these powers. He was content to demonstrate the distinction between them by the evidence of the Scriptures and to show that to place Christ in a Jewish setting was necessarily to falsify and utterly misunderstand his teaching.

Marcion therefore based his faith on St Paul, 'the first who had really understood the mission of Christ'. Many Gnostic sects claimed to be repositories of a secret teaching delivered by one or other of the Apostles. Marcion went further and said that the twelve had so misunderstood the real teaching of Christ that it had to be revealed anew to Paul. Rejecting the Jewish element in Christianity altogether, Marcion substituted for the Old Testament two Christian books, 'The Gospel' and 'The Apostle'. His Gospel was Luke, which he interpreted as a substitute for the Jewish Law and ethical code. 'The Apostle' was a collection of the Pauline epistles which seems to have included all those now regarded by modern scholars as genuine (i.e. omitting 1 and 2 Timothy, Titus, and Hebrews but including a letter called 'Laodiceans', which was almost certainly our Ephesians).

Here is a most extraordinary and significant fact which throws a great deal of light on the evolution of the New Testament and of the text which has come down to us. Marcion assigned the highest possible authority to Paul and treated his letters as Holy Scripture *par excellence*. Yet in the form in which we have these letters (and also the Gospel of Luke) they contain passages which flatly contradict the well-known views of Marcion and his disciples. Professor Lake says (*The Making of the New Testament*, p. 99):

It is generally argued that Marcion revised the text to suit his own ideas of the truth, but it is not certain that the Catholic text does not contain changes made in opposition to Marcion, and possibly to other heretics, and this question has never been adequately studied. The nature of a Catholic and a heretic in those days was not so different that the one may be supposed to have emended the text often and the other never. This is not due to dishonesty, but to the character of minds and manuscripts. Every mind, Catholic or heretic, was convinced (a) that he knew the truth, (b) that the truth was contained in Scripture. But it was conceded that every manuscript was written by a scribe prone to error, for though the Holy Spirit guided the authors of the New Testament it did not protect the scribes who copied it. Therefore, when anyone, Catholic or heretic, found a statement in the New Testament which appeared to be wrong, it would seem to him a moral duty to correct an obvious scribal error into a true statement. But who can say what are the limits of scribal errors?

The copying of manuscripts by hand was bound to lead to a large number of scribal errors, especially as the Christians were a poor and illegal society and most of the scribes were amateurs. Words drop out, get reinserted in the margin, and thus change their places in the sentence and alter their meanings. A reading contrary to orthodox ideas, once accidentally omitted, would lead thereafter to the belief that it was a heretic interpolation and therefore to its continued omission, while familiarity with comparable passages elsewhere would lead to unconscious assimilation of texts where the wording differed. It was not until the latter part of the fourth century that the Greek text was standardized. When, therefore, appeal is made to the New Testament as ultimate authority for the Christian faith it must be remembered that its text and contents did not assume their final form and sacrosanct quality until a comparatively late date, and that prior to this the books composing them had been in circulation and subject to this process of revision and 'correction' for a period of something like two hundred years. In fact, as Burkitt tells us, it was, ironically enough, Marcion who formally 'canonized' the Pauline Epistles. The rival Church which he founded lasted for centuries and it is to Marcion's organization of a separate Church that Runciman traces the divergence between orthodox Christianity and that dualist stream which led via

Paulicians and Bogomils to the Cathars. Like Marcion, the Paulicians revered the Apostle Paul but, as Toynbee has shown, their name was more probably derived from Paul of Samosata.

This Paul was bishop of Antioch (260–72) during a period of crisis for the Roman Empire when a great part of the Middle East was ruled from Palmyra by Odenathus and his celebrated wife Zenobia. Paul taught that Jesus was human by nature but that he was deemed worthy to receive a fuller measure of the Divine Spirit than any other man. This view, known as Adoptionism, was condemned by a synod of bishops and Paul was declared deposed. But the sentence could not be carried out until the Emperor Aurelian had captured Antioch from Zenobia. On being appealed to by the 'catholic' party, Aurelian ruled that, since the bishops of Italy had pronounced against Paul, he must relinquish the temporal possessions of his office. Thus, even before the official toleration of Christianity, the Roman government was favouring unity through centralization, and this imperial policy became more marked in the next century when Christianity became the established religion of the Empire. Not only were pagans discriminated against but heretics too. The Great Ecumenical Councils, Nicea (325), Constantinople (381), Ephesus (431), and Chalcedon (451), defined the faith ever more rigidly. Consequently the 'heresies' could survive only outside the Empire or in remote and isolated communities within it. Their writings survive only in the most fragmentary and distorted forms and their beliefs often have to be deduced from the polemics of their adversaries. The adherents of Paul of Samosata were known as Pauliani, under which name they were condemned by the Council of Nicea, but outside the Empire they survived in Armenia, where they were known as Paulikiani, an Armenian derogatory diminutive from which Toynbee, following Conybeare, derives the name Paulician.

The Paulician revival led by Constantine Silvanus arose in the chaotic period of the seventh century when the Roman (now called Byzantine) Empire was losing most of its Middle East territories to the Islamic advance. Constantine's Paulicians undoubtedly included many surviving heretic fragments which were consolidated by him into a unified movement.

After the overthrow of this movement its survivors in their turn— those of whom were not transferred to the Balkans—lingered on in Armenia where Dr Conybeare found them in the last century and published their documentary material in *The Key of Truth* (Oxford, 1898). In this text the Paulicians call themselves 'the holy, universal and apostolic church'. Conybeare confidently asserted that this is what in truth they were, the real heretics being the Incarnationists.

We have outlined then, the triumph of the Catholic or Incarnationist tradition over one of the possible alternative forms which Christianity might have taken. We have seen that this alternative appears to be derived in great part from Marcion and from Paul of Samosata. But what about its claim to be the true Apostolic Church? The wording of the Paulician baptism ceremony, like the Catharist Consolamentum, implies a tradition anterior to Marcion. The evidence we can find for such a tradition is necessarily speculative and hypothetical, but not inconsiderable. History, it has been well said, is written by the winners, and the losers must make the best they can of the meagre and fragmentary evidence left to them. With this proviso, let us see what we can discern of an even earlier Christian tradition.

13

The Alternative Tradition

As A RESULT of the exile in Babylon, Israel had been transformed from a nation into a 'Church' whose characteristic institution was the synagogue, with religious duties enshrined in the observance of the Law as expounded by the Scribes and Pharisees, while in Jerusalem the Sadducees maintained the restored Temple worship. It is often forgotten, however, that it was only the kingdom of Judah which had been taken captive by Nebuchadnezzar in 586 BC. The kingdom of Israel had been overthrown long before by the Assyrians. Seven centuries of recurrent anarchy and successive conquests, accompanied by migrations and population changes, had produced an incredible amalgamation of peoples, cultures, and religions in the whole area of what is now Syria, Lebanon, and Palestine. Over all there was a Hellenistic veneer, particularly in the cities, but the countryside largely retained its Semitic flavour and the language of the people was Aramaic. Survivals of older religious observances were everywhere to be found, notably the worship of local deities on the 'high places', denounced so often by the Old Testament prophets, while the Samaritans still worshipped Jehovah on Mount Gerizim (John 4: 20) and claimed that it was they, not the Judaeans, who had preserved the true traditions of Israel.

The province of Galilee was in many ways a perfect epitome of this Levantine amalgam of Hellenized orientalism, but it had a more Hebraic flavour than its neighbouring provinces such as Samaria, Ituraea, or Decapolis. It is Galilee which is generally thought to have been the home of much of the apocalyptic literature, and it was certainly in Galilee that it enjoyed its greatest vogue. On the other hand, as is apparent in the New Testament, the Galileans were despised as ignorant and heretical rustics by the Judaeans. But it was to these Galileans that the message of Jesus was primarily addressed, and it was by them that it was enthusiastically received. When he went to Jerusalem—where, so far as we know, he spent only one week of his active life—he came into a very different atmosphere.

In his monograph *The Dead Sea Scrolls and Christian Origins* (S.P.C.K., London, 1969) Matthew Black says:

This creative and fluid period in Judaism is one which can only be adequately characterized as that of a widespread and vigorous Jewish sectarianism, a kind of Jewish non-conformity, opposed to the official (predominantly Pharisaic) Judaism of Jerusalem, centred on the Temple and the Jerusalem Sanhedrin. It was represented in the North by strongly anti-Jerusalem, anti-Pharisaic Samaritan groups (Galilee fell well within the sphere of influence of these powerful Samaritan sectaries). In the South its best known representative was the monastic or semi-monastic sect of the Essenes, located by the ancient historians at the Dead Sea, and quite certainly to be identified with the sect of the scrolls. These were fissiparous groups, but they were solidly united in their opposition to the Judaism of Jerusalem; and they had much in common—Samaritan type Pentateuchs, e.g. have been found at Qumran, and patristic evidence locates a group of Essenes in Samaria. The strong probability is that these anti-Jerusalem sectaries were the descendants of the remnant Israel of the period of the Exile.

This brings us to consideration of the Essenes whom we mentioned briefly earlier. Until recently the main source of information on the Essenes has been Josephus, the Jewish historian who was one of the generals of the Jews in the great revolt of AD 66–70, and who subsequently went over to the Romans. In recent years this information has been supplemented by the discoveries known as the Dead Sea Scrolls, many of which seem to be Essene documents.

The subject is controversial, but certain points seem to be clear. First, the term Essene covers a fairly wide spectrum and is not to be confined only to those extremely ascetic communities in the desert and around the Dead Sea about which we have documentary evidence. Josephus tells us that the Essenes formed colonies in every city and their numbers were to be reckoned in thousands. Professor Dupont-Sommer in his book *The Jewish Sect of Qumran and the Essenes* says: 'All Judea, both in the towns, including Jerusalem, and in the villages, was honeycombed with these many Essene settlements, each of which spread around itself an atmoshere of mysticism and carried out a programme of propaganda'; whilst Dr Black remarks: 'It is from this side of Judaism that Christianity took its origins' and, in a striking phrase, says, 'Essenism is the larval stage of Christianity.'

From what Josephus has to tell us on the Essenes the following points of contact with Christ's teaching are noteworthy:

1. They had to sell all they had and give to the poor or put the money in a common treasury, as described in Acts 5: 32.

2. Their preachers never carried money, food or spare clothing because a member of the sect in every town they went to would supply their needs (cf. Mark 6: 8).

3. They aimed to be meek and lowly in spirit, pure in heart, and merciful to all men, to hate the sin but reclaim the sinner.

4. Their yea was to be yea and their nay, nay. No oaths.

5. Their highest degrees of holiness were: to become the Temple of the Holy Spirit by purity and then, finally, to acquire the power to perform miraculous cures and cast out evil spirits (cf. Mark 9: 29, 'this kind can come forth by nothing but by prayer and fasting').

Certain features, too, remind us irresistibly of Catharism. It is clear that, like the Cathars, the Essenes were divided into those who had taken full obligations and lived in community and those who lived in the world, while their common meals were sacramental in character. One who wished to enter their society passed first through a period of probation and when received was given a girdle and a white robe. Of their doctrine Josephus says (*Wars*, Bk. 2, Ch. 8) that bodies are corruptible and that the matter they are made of is not permanent, but that souls are immortal, that they come out of the most subtle air and are united in their bodies as in prisons, into which they are drawn by a certain natural enticement; but that when they are set free from the bonds of the flesh, they then, as released from a long bondage, rejoice and mount upward.

The Romano-Jewish War of 66–70, culminating in the fall of Jerusalem and the destruction of the Temple, had a devastating effect on both the established Jewish religion and nascent Christianity. The Christian Church had been born at Jerusalem and the 'Church of the Apostles and Elders' there had been regarded as the Mother Church. They had remained entirely Jewish, continuing the Temple worship and differing from other Jews only in the belief that Jesus w. ᵗ the Messiah and that his return in glory was imminent. But, as a re˹ ˎ˹ the war, the Jerusalem Church removed in 67 to Pella in Decapol. Here it found itself in a totally different atmosphere. All over Galilee, Decapolis, and southern Syria there were large numbers of people on whom Christ had made a profound impression simply by his teaching and his personality. These were the *ebionim*, the 'poor in spirit' of the Beatitudes. Another Beatitude is addressed to the 'pure in heart'—*oi katharoi te kardia*. Ginsburg lists *katharoi* as one of the etymologies of the word Essene. Moreover, at Pella, as Beveridge tells us, 'the Church was recruited from the Essenes and an Essene element began to penetrate it'. It is an interesting suggestion that the relationship of the ebionim to the Essenes was perhaps analogous to that of the Cathar Credents to the Perfecti. After the first century the Essenes are no longer heard of and it seems a reasonable assumption that they were simply absorbed in the nascent Christian Church, or indeed, were its nucleus.

It must be borne in mind that the Acts of the Apostles, which is virtually our only source of information on the earliest days of the

Church, deals almost exclusively with the activities of Peter and Paul. It does, nevertheless, incidentally reveal that there were already Christian communities in many cities before they are referred to in Acts. Who, for example, were the disciples in Damascus whom St Paul went to extirpate and by whom he was received after his conversion? The whole episode, from his healing by Ananias to his escape from the city, shows that this must have been an organized and well-established community. At Antioch, too, there was already a Church, and St Luke tells us (Acts 13: 1) that among the prophets and teachers there was 'Manaen which had been brought up with Herod the tetrarch' Josephus in the *Antiquities of the Jews* (Book XV) also tells of a certain Essene named Manahem, much esteemed by Herod, who was celebrated as a prophet and a man of holy life, that he and Herod had been boys together, and that while going to school he had told Herod that he would one day be king.

After the fall of Jerusalem Christianity developed in two distinct cultural regions. The first was the Aramaic and Syriac speaking area stretching northwards from Palestine to the region of Antioch and beyond to the Taurus mountains. The second was the Hellenistic, largely Greek-speaking region of Asia Minor that was the mission field of St Paul. It was this latter which developed Catholic Christianity, but it is in the former, much less well documented, that we must seek the origins of the alternative tradition. It was in this region that the earliest Christian writings circulated. Written in Aramaic, they preceded the existing New Testament canon, but none of them survive intact today. Aramaic was a provincial tongue while Greek was universal. It was inevitable, therefore, that when the Church became international its local Aramaic writings were absorbed and adapted; not only was the language changed, but the original content was modified to fit the emerging Catholic consensus.

One of these Aramaic documents was a collection of the Sayings of Jesus which tradition attributed to the Apostle Matthew. These have been incorporated into, and probably gave their name to, the present Gospel according to St Matthew, which was written in Greek, probably in the region of Antioch, around AD 80. They form what is usually referred to as the Sermon on the Mount; but this Gospel in Greek was preceded by a Gospel according to the Hebrews, written in Aramaic, or perhaps in Hebrew. St Jerome, writing about AD 400, tells us, 'I had an opportunity of copying it afforded me by the Nazarenes who use the book, at Beroea, a city of Syria'. Beroea is the modern Aleppo. Epiphanius, in his work against Heresies, says, 'The Ebionites use the Gospel according to Matthew. This they too, like the followers of Cerinthus, use to the exclusion of others, and they call it according to the Hebrews.' He goes on to say that he had heard of Hebrew versions of John and Acts kept privately in the treasuries at Tiberias.

Two significant variations from the received Gospels are noted by St Jerome, Origen, Epiphanius, and all who have seen this Gospel. First, at the baptism of Jesus, the words from Heaven are: 'Thou art my beloved son . . . this day have I begotten thee.' That this is the original wording is shown also by the fact that it is these words that are cited by St Paul in his preaching (Acts 13: 34). Secondly, in the Lord's prayer, says Jerome, 'for supersubstantial bread I found mahar, which means "of the morrow" . . . it is thus: our bread of the morrow give us this day; that is, the bread which thou wilt give us in thy kingdom, give us this day.' Here we have in first-century Palestine two of the most distinctive features of thirteenth-century Catharism. Scholars also believe that the Oxyrhynchus Sayings are extracts from the Hebrew Gospel, in which case the following reconstruction by Stephen Caiger (*Archaeology and the New Testament*) of a fragmentary passage is highly significant for the light it throws on the real teaching of Jesus: 'The kingdom of Heaven is within you and whosoever shall know himself shall find it. Strive therefore to know yourselves and ye shall be aware that ye are the sons of the Almighty Father; and ye shall know that ye are in the city of God and that ye are the city.'

There is also strong linguistic evidence that there was an Aramaic original on which St John's Gospel was based. This, however, is a very controversial matter and the experts themselves disagree on it. It seems probable that the writer of the Gospel as we have it made use of an Aramaic source which had the authority of an eyewitness to the events but whose account was in other respects unsuitable for the Church of the second century, and that he edited it in such a way as to reconcile the Synoptic evangelistic tradition with Pauline Christology. As Professor Bacon put it in *The Making of the New Testament*, 'The beloved disciple is a Paul present in the spirit . . . the Pauline incarnation doctrine, formulated in terms of the Stoic and Platonic Logos theory is applied to the story of Jesus as tradition reported it.'

We are told in the eleventh chapter of Acts that it was in Antioch that the disciples were first called Christians. This was the term generally adopted throughout the Greek-speaking world, but among the Jews and Aramaic-speaking peoples they were known as Nazarenes or Ebionites. Some writers distinguish between the two terms, but their evidence is often contradictory. On the whole it would seem that the term Ebionite was applied more often to those who still held strongly to the Jewish faith and believed that it was necessary to fulfil the Law, while Nazarene was applied more generally over the Syriac world, where it survived until the fifth century. St Jerome found Nazarenes in Peraea, which is now Transjordan, where Pella is too. Pliny the Elder mentions the Nazareni as forming a tetrarchy separated from Apamea by the Orontes. This is a particularly significant reference for this is the area inhabited today by the Nosairis, otherwise known as Alawis, whose religion is the ancient pagan religion of the country modified by Christian, Moslem and, especially, Ismaili influences. A possibly significant relic of early Christianity here is the subject of the Epilogue.

One of the most interesting centres of Syriac Christianity was the city of Edessa (now Urfa), some forty miles east of the Euphrates near the present border of Turkey and Syria. Edessa was the capital of an independent kingdom called Osrhoene, inhabited since the time of Alexander the Great by a mixed race of Greeks, Arabs, Armenians, and Syrians. Edessa claimed to have been Christian since the time of Christ himself and Eusebius quotes the letters alleged to have been exchanged between Jesus and King Abgarus of Edessa. In response to the King's request for healing, Jesus sent him a linen cloth with his features impressed on it. This cloth lay undiscovered for 500 years until it was found in a niche of a wall and it saved the city when it was besieged by the Persians. Later still, it was claimed that the Crusaders had found the famous Turin shroud at Edessa. After the Ascension, the Apostle Thaddeus was sent to Edessa in accordance with Christ's promise to King Abgarus. Conybeare tells us that, according to an early Armenian tradition, they were evangelized by St Bartholomew, who was martyred in the area of Lake Van. The traditional succession of bishops in this area goes back to Bartholomew and Thaddeus. Burkitt conjectures that Eusebius thought that Thaddeus was Addai (who may have been Tatian, a disciple of Justin Martyr) who ordained a certain Palut, later Bishop of Edessa. Although Palut was not consecrated such until about 180, nevertheless it is clear that there was here an independent Syriac-speaking Church outside the Roman Empire. Osrhoene was not annexed to the Empire until 215 and an accidentally preserved notice of a flood at Edessa in 201 mentions 'the temple of the Christians' as an important building.

Round about the year 180 a famous philosopher and astrologer called Bardaisan, a friend of King Abgar IV of Osrhoene, became a Christian. He promulgated a cosmogony which was one of the formative elements of Manichaeism. He places the 'Fall' before the creation of the world—in fact he sees the Creation as a means of redeeming those portions of the light which have been imprisoned by Darkness. 'God places in the soul the Leaven, a divine faculty which works by inherent energy till the whole soul becomes Divine.'

A most significant Syriac Christian was a certain Aphraates who was head of a convent near the modern Mosul dedicated to Mar Mattai (St Matthew). Between 337 and 345 he wrote a series of Discourses on the Faith in answer to an enquirer.

Aphraates appears to divide Christians into the 'Sons of the Covenant' and the Penitents. The Penitent is the general adherent, who has not as yet volunteered for the sacramental life; the son (or daughter) of the Covenant is the baptized Christian, who is admitted to partake of the Eucharist. Those who volunteer for baptism are to be warned—'He whose heart is set to the state of matrimony, let him marry before baptism, lest he fall in the spiritual contest and be killed . . . He that hath not offered himself and hath not yet put on his armour, if he turn back he is not blamed.' In other words, the average Christian of this community looked forward to becoming a full Church member only at a somewhat advanced age, and as a prelude to retiring morally and physically from the life of this world. In Aphraates, baptism is not the common seal of every Christian's faith, but a privilege reserved for celibates, or at least for those who intended to live a celibate life for the future. We meet with a similar organization among the Marcionites and the Manichees [*op. cit.* p. 499].

And, need we add, among the Cathars of Languedoc?

Once Catholic Christianity had become the official religion of the Roman Empire 'heretics' such as these were 'reconciled' to the 'Church' or survived only precariously in remoter and more backward places. Rabbula, Bishop of Edessa 411–35, made great efforts in this direction and also replaced the Diatessaron of Tatian, which had been the 'Scripture' of the Syriac-speakers, by a Syriac translation of the now canonical New Testament. But, of early Syriac-speaking Christianity, Burkitt (*Early Eastern Christianity*, 1904) notes that it 'is the nearest thing we can get to . . . a history of the Church as it might have been had its environment been different' and 'It is a real and serious question how much of the expression of our religion is conditioned not by Divine revelation, but by the effort to fit it into the philosophical ideas current at the time when Christian theology became articulate.'

142

14

The Real Gospel?

A RESTATEMENT of Christianity in terms acceptable to the spirit of the age is a need which is widely felt at the present time. The problem is to find the warrants which could give validity to such a restatement. If the traditional statement is to be discarded, by what authority can another be substituted?

Theology is the science of God, a rationalization based on the human experience of the divine. Whether the experience is valid is one thing; whether the rationalization built upon that experience is logical and acceptable to reason is quite another. It is the obscuring of this distinction which lies at the root of the problem. Religious experience does not occur in a vacuum; its meaning is inevitably conditioned by the nature of the mind in which it occurs. What applies to an individual applies also to the experience of the race. If the revelation of God in Jesus Christ was the supreme religious experience of Christendom, it nevertheless occurred as a historical event at a particular time in the world's history. It needed therefore to be interpreted in terms of the prevailing ideas, hopes, beliefs, expectations, and psychological climate.

The psychological climate in which the Gospel was born was dominated by two outstanding ideas: among the Jews of Palestine, apocalyptic Messianism: in the Hellenistic world, the idea of mystical regeneration by sacramental participation in the sacrificial death of a redeemer-god. The influence of these two conceptions on emergent Christianity was decisive and inevitably provided the framework in which any divine manifestation had to be placed in order to secure acceptance. We have already noted the remarkable fact that these two ideas are, to all appearance, mutually contradictory. It was the religious genius of St Paul that found the reconciling synthesis in the doctrine of the Atonement. Out of the impact of the historic experience of the Incarnation upon the psychological climate of the age as interpreted by the genius of St Paul, and subsequently developed by St Augustine, the whole edifice of Christian theology has been built. But theology is nothing more than the intellectual wrapping in which spiritual experience has to be dressed if it is to be communicated. Now that the psychological climate has changed, a religious presentation that was admirably adapted to its period seems more and more to lack meaning.

The cultured Hellenes who found religious satisfaction in the Mystery schools could no more return to the primitive vegetation rites out of which they had grown than modern man can now accept the framework in which the Christian revelation was originally dressed. Many now find the doctrine of original sin and vicarious atonement incomprehensible and are repelled by such imagery as 'washed in the blood of the Lamb'. As for the old-fashioned eschatology, with its heaven above and its hell below, the dreadful Day of Judgement with angels blowing trumpets on the clouds, the resurrection of the dead with their bodies, the eternal damnation of the wicked, and the rest— all this we find grotesque and absurd. Almost everyone now recognizes that such conceptions belong to the museum; but so long as the Church is unable to consign them there she will be unable to provide that restatement of religion which is today demanded. More seriously, so long as the Church remains committed to presenting the Christian revelation in terms of dead ideas and an obsolete view of the universe, thousands are being repelled who would draw nigh to Christ. This obsolete framework hangs like a millstone round the neck of Christian orthodoxy, denying to it all hope of ever bringing the heavenly bread to the millions who are starving for the want of it.

This, of course, is perfectly well realized by the accredited guardians of the Christian revelation; but so long as they are content simply to gloss over these uncomfortable antiquities, interpreting them allegorically or symbolically, and refuse to recognize that they are nothing more than obsolete theological machinery then the Church will continue to be guilty of intellectual dishonesty and official religion will go on evaporating into a vague ethical humanitarianism which has lost all sense of its basis in religious experience.

The real difficulty is that orthodoxy dare not allow the old framework to be discarded entirely, for if it does what becomes of Christ? Can the statement that Jesus is the Son of God have any meaning or significance in any other framework than the one in which it has been embedded? And if it can, by what authority is the restatement to be made?

Perhaps what we have called the 'Alternative Tradition' can help towards a solution of this dilemma. Like the orthodox tradition, it has accumulated many accretions and aberrations down the centuries, but it has retained throughout certain distinctive characteristics that are perfectly compatible, not only with the modern *weltanschauung*, but with both the teaching and the divinity of Christ.

First, as Aphraates taught, Christianity is 'the revelation of a divine spirit dwelling in man and fighting against moral evil'. Christ is not an atoning sacrifice but a forerunner and an exemplar; enlightenment, not redemption, is his mission. He is the first of a new type—not God who became man, but a human person who took on the divine nature and showed the way for all men to follow.

Secondly, Christianity is a life to be lived rather than a dogma to be believed. What is wrong with the world is that man has forgotten his divine nature; when he remembers it he will be saved (literally, 'brought safe home')—for salvation is from ignorance, not from sin. Christ (or 'Good men') saves from this ignorance.

Thirdly, there is the distinction between the Elect and the Hearers; the setting apart of an élite who model themselves on Christ and in some sense become Christ, receiving the baptism of the Holy Spirit as he did. To quote Aphraates again: 'Man was formed by Him in His own image to be a Temple for Him to dwell in'. And as Bardaisan of Edessa said, 'God places in the soul the Leaven, a divine faculty which works by inherent energy till the whole soul becomes divine.'

Finally, there is one small detail, unimportant in itself, but of immense significance as evidence of continuity from the Essenes of Christ's own day right through to the Cathars of thirteenth-century Languedoc: the girdle which the Elect, the Perfectus, put on at his initiation.

So what of the teaching of Christ in the light of this?

It is quite evident that the first believers and the apostles themselves identified Jesus with that Son of Man who should come in clouds at the end of the age to judge the world. But did Jesus himself share that view? Was he a mere victim of his environment, or had he a different and distinctive teaching of his own? It is impossible to read the Gospels with a knowledge of the background which the Book of Enoch provides without realizing at once that he had, and that the Evangelists have put into his mouth words quite foreign to his own distinctive conception. There is nothing really shocking or surprising in this. Those who believed Jesus to be the promised Messiah inevitably, and quite unconsciously, attributed everything in the popular Messianic conception to him. The Evangelists were writing half a century later when the sayings of Jesus had been handed down by word of mouth among a body of men fanatically imbued with this distinctive view of the meaning of his revelation. Even so, it is worth noting that Mark, the earliest of the Gospels, has only 28 passages of Apocalyptic matter against 132 in Matthew and 178 in Luke and Acts.

It is obvious, therefore, that the original and distinctive teaching of Jesus is not to be sought in any of those passages which merely reflect or are deeply coloured by apocalyptic thought. But there are many places where we find ideas flatly contradictory to it attributed to him, which often make nonsense of the context in which they occur. Given the circumstances, the only way in which the retention of these passages can be accounted for is that they represented what he actually did say. That Jesus had to take into account the psychological atmosphere of his time and frame his teaching accordingly is only what we should expect. But again and again we find him using this background and interpreting it afresh with a characteristic twist. Wherever we find this we can feel sure that we have a genuine record of Jesus' own teaching and not a mere apocalyptic echo put into his mouth. An admirable example of this is the picture of the sheep and the goats in the twenty-fifth chapter of Matthew.*

He starts with a picture well known to his hearers from the 63rd chapter of 1 Enoch, describing the Son of Man sitting on the throne of his glory and all the nations being gathered together before him to be judged. The picture drawn by Enoch then goes on: 'And all the kings and the mighty . . . will supplicate for mercy at his hand. Nevertheless the angels of punishment will take them in charge to execute vengeance upon them because they have oppressed his children and His elect. And they will be a spectacle for the righteous and for His elect, and the righteous and the elect will be saved on that day. The kings and the mighty . . . descend into the flame of the pain of Sheol.'

But Jesus, using this picture so familiar to his hearers, makes the king say to those who are accepted: 'I was hungered and ye gave me meat; I was thirsty and ye gave me drink; I was a stranger and ye took me in; naked and ye clothed me; I was sick and ye visited me; I was in prison and ye came unto me . . . inasmuch as ye have done it unto one of the least of these my brethren, ye have done it unto me.' And those who are rejected are those who have not done these things, who have failed to recognize God in their fellow men, and not merely the oppressors of the chosen people. The codicil about their going away into everlasting punishment is merely the apocalyptic completion of the original picture and can safely be rejected as 'unchristian' in the truest sense of the word. For wherever we find characteristic apocalyptic imagery and wording attributed to Jesus we can do more than hazard a guess that it is not his own original teaching, we can in fact safely assume that it is not. On the other hand, whenever we find him flatly contradicting it or subtly introducing a new conception into that

*I am indebted for this to T. H. Brindley, *Religious Thought in Palestine in the Time of Christ* (Methuen, 1931).

framework—a conception usually hopelessly misunderstood by his hearers—then we can say with certainty, 'This is the real Jesus.' For there are passages in the Synoptic Gospels which stand in sharp contrast and contradiction to the general tone. These can only have been retained because they were actually remembered as having been spoken by Jesus. When we extract and classify these passages we find that they present two distinctive features. The first is a conception of the kingdom, or reign of God, as purely spiritual and inward, a matter of becoming, not something visible and tangible which suddenly arrives at a particular moment in time. To an audience which was looking for a visible kingdom of God which should come in the clouds of heaven with great glory to the accompaniment of angel trumpets, Jesus says: 'The kingdom of Heaven cometh not with observation ['is not coming as you hope to catch sight of it' in Moffat's version], neither shall they say, Lo here! or Lo there! for behold, the kingdom of God is within you.' (Luke 17: 20.)

In all his characteristic teaching on the nature of this kingdom, or reign of God, Jesus is striving to implant in his hearers a conception which is poles apart from the current materialistic idea of a spectacular supernatural event or an automatic reward which the righteous can passively await. On the contrary he tells them they must seek it (Matt. 6: 33). It is not something to be conferred in the future; it has come already, it is present now in their very midst (Matt. 12: 28), and they can start now to 'lay up treasure' there (Matt. 6: 20). It is the divine potentiality within man, a hidden treasure (Matt. 13: 44), a pearl of great price, to obtain which everything else must be sacrificed (Matt. 13: 45–6). And it is also a growing and a becoming, a transforming potency. He compares it to a seed which has been sown and is growing secretly (Mark 4: 26–9); starting as the tiniest of seeds it will yet grow into a great tree (Mark 4: 30–2, Matt. 13: 31–2). Although tares and weeds may be growing with it (Matt. 13: 24–30) yet it has within it the power to transform all that it touches, 'like leaven which a woman took and hid in three measures of meal till the whole was leavened' (Matt. 13: 33).

How strikingly this is brought out in the parable of the talents!. Notice how this parable is introduced in Luke's Gospel (Luke 19: 11f). 'He spake a parable, *because* he was nigh to Jerusalem, and *because* they thought that the kingdom of God should immediately appear. He said *therefore* . . .' The parable of the talents follows, to drive home yet once more that the kingdom is to be attained by making the best use of what we have already, by the growth of the seed which has been implanted, by the fructifying of the hidden treasure. The unprofitable servant is the one who fails to make use of his endowment, of the divine potentiality within him. And his punishment is to lose it. 'To him that hath shall be given.' In Mark's Gospel, which however, has omitted the parable, these words 'to him that hath shall be given, etc' are immediately followed by the image of the seed growing secretly, which is introduced by the word, '*So*'. '*So* is the kingdom of God, as if a man should cast seed into the ground . . . and the seed should spring and grow up' (Mark 4: 26f). And thereupon follows the parable of the mustard seed.

The second distinctive feature of the teaching of Jesus which contrasts sharply with the prevailing ideas, and which the most superficial reading of the Gospels shows to have been completely misunderstood by his contemporaries, is his conception of the suffering and death of the Messiah. This was absolutely inconceivable to the Jew of that, or indeed any, period. The Messiah they looked for was a glorious being who should come on the clouds in majesty and power to judge the world as God's viceregent, or alternatively a triumphant heir of David who should restore the kingdom of Israel and subdue all the nations of the earth to his victorious sway. The idea that he must first die a shameful death after being 'despised and rejected of men' was utter blasphemy to a pious Jew. And it was for precisely that reason that the Jews rejected Jesus.

There can be no doubt whatever that the identification of the promised Messiah with the suffering servant of Jahveh spoken of by Isaiah (ch. 53) was an absolutely original and revolutionary conception of Jesus himself. It is quite certain that never, prior to this time, had the suffering servant been identified with the Messiah. To the Jews the suffering servant was, and still is, the whole Chosen People. Isaiah himself expressly identifies him with the whole people of Israel, or at the very least with the faithful remnant. (Isaiah 44: 21, 49: 3–6). On the other hand, when Isaiah speaks of the Lord's Christ in the same context he applies that title to Cyrus, King of Persia (Isaiah 45: 1).

Isaiah (ch. 41) accepted the suffering, and even the symbolic death, of the nation, abandoning the earlier hope of a glorious restoration of Zion and accepting the dispersion of the Jews as part of the purpose of God, as indicating for them a missionary destiny to the whole earth. But Jesus goes further. He clearly, deliberately, and of set purpose destroyed the last surviving hope of his people's traditional national and religious belief. While not rejecting the title of Messiah, he deliberately took Isaiah's picture of the rejected and suffering servant out of its context and applied it to himself. His disciples were dumbfounded and scandalized. When they hailed him as the Christ (Mark 8: 29) 'He charged them that they should tell no man' (Mark 9: 10); and then, *immediately*, 'He began to teach them that the Son of Man must suffer many things and be rejected . . . (Mark 9: 32). Peter, who had just hailed him as Christ, 'began to rebuke him'! (Luke 11: 45). On every single occasion in the Gospels when Jesus refers to his coming death the evangelists tells us candidly, 'They understood not that saying' (Luke 18: 34).

Jesus never said publicly that he was the Messiah and this was clearly felt as a difficulty by the first preachers of the Gospel. Peter's explanation was that he had revealed it privately to the Apostles and told them not to reveal it till he had risen. Yet these are the very passages where the Apostles are represented as failing to understand; it is obviously post hoc reasoning on their part. Even Jesus's reply to the High Priest's direct question (Matt. 26: 64) may only mean, 'That is your statement, not mine.'

So why does he deliberately court death? There was no practical alternative. Having arrived at Jerusalem he was hailed as the Messiah. The whole authority behind his teaching, which had made a colossal impression, was this belief. He must do something decisive and yet not inconsistent with that belief. He could not preach all his life. He could not simply disappear or go into retirement. If he denied Messiahship in any way the whole movement which he had built up would collapse—he would be dismissed as just another imposter, of whom there had been so many at that time. Yet, equally obviously, he could not satisfy the popular expectation of the Messiah. Therefore, the only thing he could do was deliberately to give a new interpretation of the Messianic function by linking it to the suffering servant idea and to demonstrate, in the most dramatic manner possible, that the Christ was not a conquering king. He thereby also lived his own teaching and illustrated perfectly the nature of God—giving Himself utterly.

There is a spiritual or divine quality in the universe which man possesses. The nearest quality to it of which we are normally conscious is love, but it far transcends our normal conception of love. This quality is the driving force, the motive power of the universe. To 'know God' is to realize and experience this quality in oneself, and to express it is to be divine. How is such a conception to be conveyed to people who believe in an anthropomorphic deity and who will pay no heed to anyone claiming divine revelation unless it is associated with their Messianic expectations? In his preaching Jesus tries to convey it by allegory and parable, personifying the divine life force as a heavenly father. Privately, to the disciples, when he asks them who they think he is and they answer 'the Christ', he makes the association with the suffering servant prophecies in order to prepare them for what he foresees will be the inevitable material outcome of his mission. He tries to go beyond this, but they are incapable of understanding and are afraid to ask what he meant. (Mark 9: 32)

But someone must have understood. There is a persistent tradition of an inner teaching which is associated with the 'beloved disciple' who has been given the name John but who could not possibly have been the son of Zebedee. (The Gospel called John has, as we have seen, been 'edited' in a catholic sense.) This teaching, 'the real Gospel', must have been transmitted by some sort of apostolic succession down through the ages. In the chapter on the alternative tradition we have suggested what its line of descent might have been. The evidence admittedly falls short of conclusive proof, but the wording of the Cathar ritual conveys an implication which is inescapable: 'This holy baptism by which the Holy Spirit is given, the Church of God has kept from the Apostles until now, and it has passed from "good men" to "good men" until the present, and will continue to do so until the end of the world.'

On the night before Montségur surrendered four 'good men' left the castle in secret and made the perilous descent by rope to the Lasset gorge. They would have preferred to stay and share the fate of their comrades, but they were commanded to leave in order to place 'the treasure of the church' in security. Yet on 14 June 1244, Imbert de Salas deposed before the Inquisition:

Pierre Roger had had the Cathar treasure carried away. About Christmas in particular, the deacon Matheus and his companion Bonnet took away an enormous quantity of gold and silver. The men of Camon, who formed the blockade in the Ers gorge, secretly devoted to Pierre Roger their former lord, let the sacred treasure pass. The two deacons transported it to the cave of Ornolac in the Sabarthès.

So it was no material treasure that Amiel Aicard and his companions saved from Montségur. To slide down a precipice in darkness and secrecy they could carry only themselves. But in themselves was the treasure, the power to transmit the apostolic succession, the seed perhaps of a higher form of Christianity to be revealed when the world is ready to receive it.

EPILOGUE

A Personal Reminiscence

FROM the Lebanon northwards to the Turkish border stretches a range of mountains known as the Jebel Ansariya or Alawite mountains which has been for over a thousand years the home of the Nosairi sect, named Alawites since the French occupation. In this region, extending for approximately one hundred miles along the Syrian coast and some thirty miles inland, the Nosairis form the overwhelming majority of the rural population, while the Sunni Moslems and Christians are concentrated in the small townships on the sea coast.

The Nosairis practise a secret initiatory religion whose real tenets are known only to the adepts and which it is death to disclose to the profane. No proselytism is ever practised, and in order to divert or discourage inquisitiveness it is permissible to pretend adherence to the outward forms of the prevailing religion, such outward forms being but the garment which conceals the true faith.

In its historical origins Nosairism is considered to be a branch of the Shia heresy and to have arisen in the general anarchy of the Qarmatian period. When the power of the Abbassid caliphs was declining a movement arose within Islam to throw off Arab political domination and to infuse a more mystical element into the Moslem religion. This movement had its origin in Persia, and in the political sphere it ultimately gave rise to the Fatimite caliphate, while on the doctrinal side it left its traces in the *gholat*, the secret, initiatory sects, such as the Druze, the Ismailis, and the Nosairis. Of these the Nosairis are the most extreme and the farthest removed from the Dar-al-Islam. They share the general characteristics of the Shia sects, the exaltation of Ali, the practice of secrecy and dissimulation with regard to their beliefs, and the allegorical interpretation of the Koran. In the case of the Nosairis, however, these characteristics are pushed to such an extreme as to remove them altogether from the general community of Islam. Moreover, the presence of Christian and pagan elements among their beliefs has been remarked upon by all scholars who have studied their religion—such practices as the sacramental use of wine in their ceremonies, together with candles, incense and odoriferous plants, the observance of Christmas, Epiphany, and Whitsuntide, and the veneration of Christian saints such as St George and St Matthew. Pagan survivals are even more evident in the practice, particularly among the *Amma* (the uninitiated as distinct from the *Khassa*, the chosen) of congregating for worship at the *qubbas*, characteristic white-domed shrines which are built upon the 'high places' and surrounded always by a sacred grove of evergreen oaks. Here incense is burned and invocations made to the *genius loci*.

A number of scholars, notably Massignon,[1] have contended that the Nosairis are really Christians who have been obliged to cloak their faith under a semblance of Moslem heterodoxy in order to escape persecution. This theory proved particularly attractive to the French for political reasons, and an attempt has been made to trace their origin to the Ghassaniya, a Christian-Arab feudatory kingdom which, until the Moslem invasion, held the southern frontiers of the Byzantine Empire against the Bedouin of Arabia. It is suggested that when the Moslem conquest of Syria took place the Ghassaniya migrated to the Jebel Ansariya and continued to nourish their Christian faith in a secret and disguised form among these inaccessible mountains, deriving fresh strength from the period of Crusader rule in the twelfth and thirteenth centuries. During the mandatory period the French set up the Alawite area as an autonomous territory and there were plans to separate it entirely from Syria in the same way as the then largely Christian Lebanon.

Dussaud[2] considers that the Nosairis were established in the area long before any Ghassaniya migration. He cites the references in Pliny and Jerome to Nazarenes in the area and says there is some evidence that they were also called Galileans.[3] Dussaud, however, considers that the core of their religion is pagan and that they have successively adopted a protective covering, first of Christianity and then of Islam. Toynbee[4] summarizes Dussaud's view: 'The Nosairis have travestied the Ismaili Shi'ism which forced an entry to their mountain fastnesses in the age of the Crusades by deifying Ali—but this is only an accretion—the core of their religion is a local worship more ancient than Islam or Christianity and perhaps even prior to that impact of Hellenism on the Syriac world in which Christianity and Islam originated.' The Nosairis themselves claim to derive their name from a certain ibn Nosair, an obscure partisan of one of the Shi'ite Imams. This is probably a good example of their genius for protective covering.

During the Second World War I served with the British Security Mission in Syria and for three years I was Head of Mission in Lattakia, the capital of the Alawite territory. My responsibility was Intelligence throughout the territory and particularly in the sensitive area of the Turkish frontier. This gave me a unique opportunity to study the Nosairi religion at close quarters and to establish personal relationships with its leading exponents.

Like all the aspects of religious expression we have examined in this book, the Nosairi religion is a product of its history and the impact upon it of a variety of ideologies. The remoteness and inaccessibility of much of the area has meant that ancient beliefs and ceremonies have lingered on there. Over the centuries governments have tended to ignore the mountain districts, unless the inhabitants gave trouble, in which case repression was usually brutal, especially in Ottoman times. The Nosairis therefore have learned to 'keep their heads down' and to dissimulate. Their religion is characterized by the use of allegory and symbolism in bewildering complexity, all devised to conceal esoteric inner meanings which must not be revealed to the profane. This enables them to pretend that beneath whatever traditional practices or beliefs the 'powers that be' find objectionable, their 'real' faith is whatever those powers approve of. Under these conditions it is hardly surprising that the French were able to contend that the Nosairis, whom they called Alawites, were really Christians and to plan to set them up in a state separate from Moslem Syria. Today, when the Alawites have become the ruling group in Syria (thanks to the French having created a largely Alawite army), they are of course good Moslems! It is the tragedy of the Middle East that one's politics are always held to be determined by one's religion. For this reason I found it convenient to let it be known that I was a Buddhist. This was given some plausibility by the presence of Gurkha troops in the area at the time and had the advantage, not only of enabling me to assume political impartiality, but also to decline the more rebarbative aspects of traditional Arab hospitality without giving offence. Moreover, no Nosairi had any motive for pretending to me that their religion was really Christian.

The Nosairis are divided into two main groups which we may, for convenience, call Northern and Southern. The Southern group is the preponderant one in the territory today, many of the Northerners having been taken out of Syria when the region round Antioch (Antakya) was ceded to Turkey in 1939. The Southern group more readily accepts the designation Alawite since this emphasizes their adherence to the Shia (Shi'at Ali) branch of Islam. The Northerners are noticeably less 'Islamic', and, in view of their cross-border relationships with their co-religionists in Turkey, it was with them that I was principally concerned from a security intelligence point of view. I made it my business to get to know their leaders as intimately as possible and, in particular, one of them who was said to be regarded as a manifestation of deity. I established such a close personal relationship with him that, when the war was over, he invited me to stay as a guest in his house. There, sitting on his verandah, which commanded a stupendous view of the mountains, we discussed religion in every aspect, and it was there that I received the enlightenment which had eluded me in the Pyrenees.

The two most important symbols in Nosairi religion (at least in its 'Northern' form) are Light, and the cup or chalice which contains the sacramental wine, in drinking which the worshipper says, 'I drink to the Light'. This symbolism of the cup led me to tell my host the legend of the Holy Grail. When I had finished he said, 'I am going to reveal to you the greatest secret of our religion, but you must never disclose that it was I who told you. This Grail you speak of is a symbol and it stands for the doctrine which Christ taught to John the Beloved alone. We have it still.'

It is now forty years since my friend 'took the Way of the stars' and I feel that, though I still may not name him, it is important that this revelation should be made known. The Nosairi obsession with secrecy was in the past essential to their survival, but I cannot believe that today such a revelation need be concealed. Of course, it is totally unsupported by any evidence other than my assertion. The reader must judge by what follows whether to think it credible. For me this was the final link which completed the chain I had been trying to reconstruct from the Cathars back to Christ, the culminating proof that my quest had not been in vain. Here surely, preserved like a fossil in this mountain fastness, is a precious relic of what I have called the Alternative Tradition. The Nosairis, and especially the Ghaibiya sect, which is the one I was able to study most closely, have preserved all the characteristics there listed: the idea of a divine spirit dwelling in man, of Christ as the man who realized his divinity, the potential in others to follow his example, the distinction between the hearers (*Amma*) and the elect (*Khassa*); and, finally, the putting on of a girdle which marks the Nosairi initiate as it did the Essene, the Paulician, and the Cathar.

The Northerners are themselves divided into sects and the one whose symbolism was revealed to me is known as Ghaibiya. This word is derived from the Arabic for absence and it means that God is absent or concealed from men. But although He is invisible He is yet omnipresent. It is the very Light that is His symbol which veils His presence, for the man who can raise his consciousness towards the apprehension of Godhead finds himself blinded by excess of Light. The heavenly wine is indeed offered, but he cannot take his communion unless he can find a vessel, a cup in which to receive it. A conception of God in whatever form is a vessel which can hold some portion of the Divine Light. This vessel may be anything from a material image to the most abstract of spiritual conceptions. These differ only in degree, in their capacity for holding the Light. The more closely the vessel corresponds to the divine the better it can serve as its vehicle or embodiment. Christ is more than the best of vessels: He is a living Grail. But other men can become Light-filled vessels too, according to their capacity to hold the divine essence. Christ was one who realized his Godhead in full consciousness. But he was still a man. He became God, but only in so far as a man *can* become God. He could not hold more of the Infinite than the greatest and holiest of vessels can hold. In him God was manifest to the world in the form of a man, reduced to the measure and stature of a man.

This doctrine solves a problem which had baffled me in my study of the Cathars. How was it that they held St John's Gospel, and especially its preface, in such reverence when their view of Christ was Adoptionist? The Word is the expression, not of a transcendent Person but of a transcendent quality in the universe. The ultimate reality, the Absolute, is not personal in its own nature but by personifying it we create a vehicle through which it can be expressed. This is what the Ghaibiya symbolism conveys in the idea of the 'absence' of God and of the cup in which God can be made manifest.

Because he had realized his Godhead in full consciousness Christ also realized that the individual cannot become wholly divine until all have attained that realization. He must return 'to seek and to save that which is lost'. From the very threshold of the Holy of Holies he must turn back and give himself utterly, even to the Cross. He can do no other, for he is God and that is the nature of God. God eternally gives Himself, pouring out His life that the world may be—and that again is the meaning of His 'absence'. The world's suffering is His suffering, and the world's joy is His joy. Suffering and loss is the universal law of loving creation. All creation, all activity, all motion, all progress, can spring only from selection. Selection implies rejection, and rejection implies suffering and loss. But without that suffering and loss there can be no love and no joy, and those who suffer most love most. God suffers infinitely and His love is infinite.

So we are brought back to the Cross, no longer a gibbet on which a sinless being atoned for man's iniquity, but a symbol of the Love that is Divine.

I told my host about the Cathars. He had never heard of them but he was, of course, immensely interested and we discussed at length the similarities and the differences in their respective beliefs and practices. One striking common feature is the idea of the fall of the soul condemned to wear a human body. By degrees the soul purifies itself and rises again towards God. There is a Nosairi prayer, 'Deliver us from these human forms and reclothe us in light among the stars.'

There is a mystical element in Languedocian Catharism which does not seem to owe anything to Bogomils or Paulicians. It is apparent in this imagery of Light and the stars, which is also such a notable feature of Nosairi imagery. Could it be that some Languedocian crusader or pilgrim to the Holy Land encountered, as I did, a Light-filled vessel? Could this be, perhaps, where the idea of the Holy Grail originated? At all events, it was there, high in the Nosairi mountains, under the clear stars, in intimate converse with such a one, that I finally shed the fantasies of occultism and realized the true nature of the Cathar treasure.

WALTER N. BIRKS

Notes

CHAPTER 1: FROM CATHARS TO NEO-CATHARS

1 As quoted in Raymond Escholier and Maurice Gardelle, *The Secret of Montségur* (Stuart, 1955). This, it should be stressed, is a work of fiction.

2 Daisy Wilmer, 'The Cathari: Their Religious and Industrial Work', in *The Occult Review*, Vol. 27, No. 5 (May 1918), 256–65.

3 For example, by Eugène Aroux, in *Les Mystères de la Chevalerie* (1858). The connection is also implied in Mrs Cooper-Oakley's *Traces of a Hidden Tradition in Masonry and Medieval Mysticism* (1900).

4 The full title of the association was *Les Amis de Montségur et du Saint-Graal, de Sabarthez et d'Occitanie* (Association d'Études Littéraires, Historiques, Archéologiques et Mystiques).

CHAPTER 3: GADAL

1 This was Gadal's account of Garrigou. It is given in Rinderknecht's appendix to the German edition of Madaule's *The Albigensian Crusade* (see the Select Bibliography).

2 *Histoire de la Magie* (1860), p. 444. Lévi (Alphonse Louis Constant) states that he gives the words as reported to him by an eyewitness who had heard them: 'Nous tenons celles que nous donnons ici d'un vieillard qui les a entendues'. The term 'Jacques' simply denoted a peasant.

3 Gadal, *Ussat-les-Bains. La Cathédrale et les 3 Eglises des Cathares Albigeois* p. 15. Translation by Walter Birks. The names given to the caves were not known in the district before M. Gadal used them; the Abbé Mir, who had been curé of Ornolac since 1913, had never heard the Bethlehem cave so called by anyone except M. Gadal. A lengthy description of the process of initiation is given in Gadal's *Sur le Chemin du Saint-Graal* (1960).

CHAPTER 4: ROCHÉ

1 See Bernadac, *Le Mystère Otto Rahn*, p. 59. Guirdham, in *The Great Heresy*, p. 114, wrongly attributes this popular title to Roché.

2 Arnaud was not alone in believing the Pog to be hollow. In 1934 the concert pianist Walter Rummel announced his theory that Montségur was the Grail Castle, stating that 'it is commonly believed huge temples and immense halls are contained in the mountain'.

3 Niel, *Les Cathares de Montségur,* 1973. Chapter 3, pp. 84 ff.

4 Bernadac, *op cit.,* p. 110 'Il avait un fort accent allemand'.

5 He had fair hair and extraordinarily pale eyes. The natives saw him simply as fat: 'un homme assez gros' (Bernadac, *op cit.,* p. 110).

6 One of them, a large boxer, was recalled by the inhabitants of Ussat. They do not seem to have liked it.

7 This had been written in 1929 although it was not published until 1960 when it appeared under the title of *Sur le Chemin du Saint Graal.*

8 In 1944, on 16 March, Gadal, Mandement and others made a pilgrimage to Montségur for the 700th anniversary of its fall. While they were there a German aircraft flew overhead, but the authorities seem to have wished to make sure that no more than the seven people permitted were present: they were not concerned with the significance of the date.

CHAPTER 5: FROM GADAL TO GALAAD

1 The plaque in the shape of a dove was found by Gadal in the late 1930s, and was exhibited for a time in the Cathar Museum at Castres. Its present whereabouts are unknown.

2 *Sabarthez,* 1981, p. 2 This is the brief guide in English issued by the Lectorium Rosicrucianum.

3 *ibid.* p. 3

4 Bernadac, Le Mystère Otto Rahn, p. 267 Translation by Walter Birks.

5 Van Rijckenborgh, *A New Call of the Septuple World-Brotherhood.* Haarlem, 1980.

CHAPTER 7: CATHARISM: THE HISTORICAL SETTING

1 The name *Paterini* was probably derived from the predominant place given by the Cathars to the Lord's Prayer, the 'Pater'. *Publicani*, or *Poplicani*, seem to be corruptions from Philipopoulos, the Bogomil centre in Bulgaria, or from the Paulicians.

2 It is interesting to note that St Francis of Assisi espoused Sister Poverty and began his preaching at the same time.

3 It was in one of these debates at Fanjeaux that the Miracle of the Fire, subject of the famous picture by Fra Angelico now in the Louvre, was said to have taken place. It was the custom for the opposing debaters to submit a written summary of their arguments to the jury. In this case both summaries were thrown on to a fire and, while that of Guilabert was burned, that of Dominic emerged three times from the flames unscathed. It was also at one of these debates that Guilabert is said to have made his famous reply on the Christian life, quoted above (p. 56).

4 These debates, in which every article of the faith was argued in public, and the numerous evidences of the conferring of the Consolamentum in the presence of large audiences make nonsense of the romancings of certain writers who have seen in Catharism an 'occult school' or an esoteric mystery of which the Troubadours spoke in veiled symbolism. Few literatures are

more 'profane', in the true sense of the word, than the amorous, courtly poetry of the Troubadours.

CHAPTER 8: FAITH AND DOCTRINE

1 Molinier, *Hist. de l'Inquisition dans le Midi de la France.*

2 This view of the role of John the Baptist was supported by citing Matthew 11, where he is recorded as doubting the mission of Jesus (v. 3) and where (v. 11) Jesus describes him as the greatest of the sons of women, i.e. the greatest demon, and says, 'the least in the kingdom of heaven is greater than he'. Nevertheless, we learn from Sacchoni that many of the Catharist sects, notably the Albanenses and those of Concorezo, had a more orthodox idea of John the Baptist. The idea of the entry of Jesus by the ear of the Virgin is found in ancient liturgies and among the orthodox Church Fathers. This is as far as the Book of John takes us in explaining the Catharist view of the Universe, of the origin of evil, the nature of man, and the mission of Christ. The remainder of the book is an account of the Last Judgement which is entirely orthodox, quoting verbatim for the most part from the canonical scriptures. Most critics are agreed that it has probably been diluted from another source.

CHAPTER 9: RITUAL AND AFFILIATION

1 Duchesne, *Origins of Christian Worship*, pp. 301–2.

2 Runciman acknowledges the inaccuracy of his title. He explains that he is using the term medieval churchmen would have found intelligible and natural; to him all dualists were Manichees, but of course Christian dualism and Manichaeism are separate religions. It is thanks to St Augustine that Manichaeism was the best known heresy in the Middle Ages, so that the merest hint of dualism would be immediately labelled Manichaean and everything that St Augustine said about Manichaean beliefs would be attributed to the persons so labelled. 'If Marcion had been refuted by a Father so well known and so revered as St Augustine, then "Marcionite" would have been the usual term of opprobrium.'

CHAPTER 10: THE JEWISH SETTING

1 The Son of Man is an idiomatic Aramaic expression which simply means human being. It originates in the Book of Daniel (7: 13) where Daniel sees a human being in heaven along with the symbolic beasts. This man represents the 'kingdom of the saints'; that is to say, the Chosen People..

EPILOGUE

1 *Encyclopaedia of Islam* (1936).

2 The best published account of the Nosairi religion is by René Dussaud, *Histoire et Religion des Nosairis* (Bouillon: Paris, 1900). No satisfactory account has been published in English.

3 The Arabic for Christians is Nasrani. Ansariyah is the Arabic plural of Nosairi.

4 *Study of History*, vol. 2, p. 56.

Select Bibliography

THE following bibliography should more properly be called a reading list, for it does not pretend to offer more than a guide to further reading for those who are interested in the Cathars and their background, and in the beliefs and activities of those whom we have called 'neo-Cathars'. A comprehensive bibliography of Catharism would not only be unwieldy but would also be out of place in a book designed for English readers, since much of its extensive literature is written and published in French. The more important French studies, however, are listed—especially those that provide the documentary sources for Cathar doctrine and ritual—together with the majority of English works on the Cathars. Many of these contain excellent specialized bibliographies for those who wish to read further, as do the purely historical works concerning the Albigensian Crusade. It should also be borne in mind that the categories used below are not mutually exclusive: books are listed only under the most appropriate heading, but they will often prove to be of considerable use elsewhere.

THE CATHARS

Bibliographies

Berne-Lagarde, P., *Bibliographie du Catharisme Languedocien* (Toulouse, 1957).
Thouzellier, C., Bibliography in *Catharisme et Valdéisme* (see below).

Periodicals

Cahiers d'Etude Cathares (Arques, 1949–). Quarterly.
Cahiers de Fanjeaux (Toulouse, 1966–). Annual.

Documents

Nelli, R., *Écritures Cathares . . . Textes Précathares et Cathares* (Paris, 1968). 2nd edition. Six texts translated into modern French, with critical commentary.
Thouzellier, C., *Catharisme et Valdéisme en Languedoc* (Louvain/Paris, 1969). 2nd edition. Describes and cites most documents for and against the Cathars.
——, *Un traité cathare inédit du debut du XIIIe siecle, d'apres le 'Liber Contra*

THE TREASURE OF MONTSÉGUR

Manicheos' de Durand de Huesca' (Louvain/Paris, 1961).
——, *Rituel Cathare. Introduction, texte critique, traduction et notes* (Paris, 1977).
Duvernoy, J., *Le Registre d'Inquisition de Jacques Fournier, Évêque de Pamiers (1318–1325)* (Toulouse, 1965, 3 vols.). This is the text. An annotated translation into French, edited by Duvernoy, was published at Paris in 1978, 3 vols.
Maitland, S. R., *Facts and Documents Illustrative of the History, Doctrine, and Rites of the Ancient Albigenses and Waldenses* (1832). English translations, with the Latin texts, of many Inquisition records and polemics against the Cathars.

History

(a) *General*
Duvernoy, J., *Le Catharisme* (Toulouse, 1976), vol. 2.
Nelli, R., *La Vie Quotidienne des Cathares du Languedoc au XIIIe siècle* (Paris, 1969).
Wakefield, W. L., *Heresy, Crusade and Inquisition in Southern France, 1100–1250* (1974).

(b) *The Crusade*
Rocquebert, M., *L'Épopée Cathare* (Paris, 1971).
Madaule, J., *Le Drame Albigeois et le destin Français* (Paris, 1961). English translation as *The Albigensian Crusade* (1967).
Sumption, J., *The Albigensian Crusade* (1978). By far the best work in English.

(c) *Inquisition*
Dossat, Y., *Les Crises de l'Inquisition Toulousaine au XIIIe siècle* (Bordeaux, 1959).
Guiraud, J., *Histoire de l'Inquisition au moyen âge* (Paris, 1935–8), 2 vols.
Lea, H. C., *A History of the Inquisition of the Middle Ages* (1888), 3 vols. (reprinted, 1955).

(d) *The people*
Ladurie, E. L., *Montaillou: Village Occitan de 1294 a 1324* (Paris, 1975; English translation as *Montaillou. Cathars and Catholics in a French village 1294–1324*, 1978). A superb study, based on the Inquisition records of Jacques Fournier.

Doctrines

Duvernoy, J., *Le Catharisme: la Religion des Cathares* (Toulouse, 1976), vol. 1 (for vol. 2, see 'History', above).
Runciman, Sir S., *The Medieval Manichee. A Study of the Christian Dualist Heresy* Cambridge, 1947). An important study, concerned with earlier movements as well as with the Cathars.
Soderberg, H., *La Religion des Cathares. Étude sur le Gnosticisme de la basse Antiquité et du Moyen Age* (Uppsala, 1949; reprinted New York, 1978).
Warner, H. J., *The Albigensian Heresy* (1922; vol. 2 appeared in 1929; it is concerned with the Crusade and the Inquisition).

Montségur

Niel, F., *Les Cathares de Montségur* (Paris, 1973). The author argues that Montségur was astronomically oriented for religious purposes. The second half of the book is concerned with the Cathar occupation and the siege.

162

Oldenbourg, Z., *Massacre at Montségur: A History of the Albigensian Crusade* (New York, 1961).

THE SETTING AND THE SOURCES

Gnosticism

Foerster, W., *Gnosis, a selection of Gnostic texts* (Oxford, 1972–4), 2 vols.

James, M. R., *The Apocryphal New Testament* (Oxford, 1924). Includes 'The Book of John the Evangelist', a Latin version of which was used by the Cathars.

Robinson, J. M., *The Nag Hammadi Library in English* (1977).

Rudolph, K., *Gnosis, the Nature and History of an Ancient Religion* (Edinburgh, 1983). The best modern study of the subject.

King, C. W., *The Gnostics and their Remains, Ancient and Medieval* (1887, 2nd edition). Although out of date in many respects this is still of value for its account of Gnostic symbols in works of art.

Mithraism

Cumont, F., *The Mysteries of Mithra* (Chicago, 1903; reprinted New York, 1956).

Vermaseren, M. J., *Mithras, the Secret God* (1963).

Manichaeism

Burkitt, F. C., *The Religion of the Manichees* (Cambridge, 1925; reprinted, New York, 1978).

Widengren, G., *Mani and Manichaeism* (1965).

The Alternative Tradition in Christianity

Black, M., *The Scrolls and Christianity* (1969).

Burkitt, F. C., *Early Eastern Christianity* (1904).

——— , *Cambridge Ancient History*, vol. 12, Ch. 14.

Conybeare, F. C., *The Key of Truth. A Manual of the Paulician Church of Armenia* (Oxford, 1898).

Dupont-Sommer, A., *The Jewish sect of Qumran and the Essenes* (1954).

Streeter, B. H., *The Four Gospels* (1926).

——— , *The Primitive Church* (1930).

——— , *Cambridge Ancient History*, vol. 2, pp. 281ff.

Toynbee, A., *A Study of History. Volume IV* (1939), pp. 624ff.

Bogomilism

Obolensky, D., *The Bogomils. A study in Balkan Neo-Manichaeism* (Cambridge, 1948; reprinted, Twickenham, 1972).

NEO-CATHARISM

Baigent, M., Leigh, R., Lincoln, H., *The Holy Blood and the Holy Grail* (1982). Further details of books dealing with Rennes-le-Chateau can be found in Saul, J. M., and Glaholm, J., *Rennes-le-Chateau, a Bibliography* (1985).

Bhotiva, Z., *Le Bulletin des Polaires* (Paris, 1930–[date of final issue unknown]).

Gadal, A., *Ussat-les-Bains. La Cathédrale et les 3 Eglises des Cathares Albigeois* (Pamiers, 1936).

—— , *Sur le Chemin du Saint-Graal. Les Anciens Mystères Cathares* (Haarlem, 1960).

Guirdham, A., *Catharism. The Medieval Resurgence of Primitive Christianity*. 1969.

—— , *The Cathars and Reincarnation* (1970).

—— , *We are One Another* (St Helier, 1974).

—— , *The Great Heresy* (St Helier, 1977).

Magre, M., *Magiciens et Illuminés* (Paris, 1930; English translation as *The Return of the Magi*, 1931).

Peyrat, N., *Histoire des Albigeois* (Paris, 1870–2), 3 vols. For an analysis of the story of the Cathars immured at Lombrives see Dengerma, J., *Les Cinq Cent Cathares emmurés de Lombrives* (Foix, 1967).

Rahn, O., *Kreuzzug gegen den Gral* (Freiburg, 1933; French translation as *La Croisade contre le Graal*, Paris, 1933).

Bernadac, C., *Le Mystère Otto Rahn. Du Catharisme au Nazisme* (Paris, 1978).

Rinderknecht, K., *Nachwort zum Thema der Neu-Katharer* (in *Das Drama von Albi*, Freiburg, 1964, the German translation of Madaule, *op. cit.*).

Roche, D., *Le Catharisme. Nouvelle édition* (Toulouse, 1947). This edition includes a description, with illustrations, of symbols and finds in the caves of Ornolac. It is omitted in subsequent editions.

Rolt-Wheeler, F., *Mystic Gleams from the Holy Grail* (1949).

Van Rijckenborgh, J., *A New Call of the Septuple World-Brotherhood of the Golden Rosycross* (Haarlem, 1980).

—— , *Sabarthez custos summorum* (Ussat-les-Bains, 1981). A guide to sites in and around Ussat: the Bethlehem cave, the cavern of Lombrives, the Musée Gadal, and Montségur.

Index

Some other CRUCIBLE titles . . .

The Murdered Magicians
The Templars and Their Myth
Peter Partner

The history of the Knights Templar has long been overshadowed by the cloudy circumstances in which the Order, accused of heresy and perversion, was ruthlessly suppressed by the French monarchy in the early fourteenth century.

But the dissolution of the Templars was only the beginning of a new and strange chapter in their history. In due course they became the focus of numerous beliefs based on their supposed occult powers, and by the eighteenth century the influence of the Templar myth was felt not only in the fantasies of occultists but even in the Gothic novel, with its frequent tales of monastic impropriety.

In this widely-praised study Dr Partner, as well as providing a succinct account of the rise and fall of the Templars, examines the fabrications and illusions about the history of the Order, from the Renaissance magicians to varieties of Templarism in our own time, and shows how a medieval act of political injustice grew into a modern fantasy.

'An excellent argumentative discussion . . . often original and always fascinating.' — Jonathan Sumption, *Times Literary Supplement*

'Illuminating and very well written . . . enlightening and entertaining.' — *Religious Studies Review*

Dr Peter Partner is the author of *The Lands of St Peter* (1972) and *Renaissance Rome 1500-1559* (1976), as well as of numerous articles on medieval and Renaissance history and modern Arab politics. Since 1955 he has taught at Winchester College.

The Inquisition
The Hammer of Heresy
Edward Burman

The often loosely-used term 'Inquisition' covers a complex and amorphous phenomenon of fundamental importance in the history of Western Europe. As an institution, it came into being early in the thirteenth century. Its effects are still felt today.

This panoramic study offers the general reader a description and interpretation of the Inquisition and its methods based on two essential moments in its history: the gradual establishment of the Holy Office and its dramatic reflowering three hundred years later. Such an approach shows how the Inquisition functioned as an elastic response to heretical and political pressure, and how its power was in direct proportion to specific geographical and temporal needs.

In the course of his survey Edward Burman describes the crucial role of the Dominican Order in the work of the Inquisition and demonstrates that the Franciscans — in spite of the gentle piety of their founder — were also involved in stamping out heresy. In addition he provides a wealth of fascinating detail concerning the Inquisitors' methods (including torture, confiscation of property, and the terrible trials for the dead), their manuals, the Inquisition in Italy, the Inquisition in France from the Albigensian Crusade to the burning of Joan of Arc, the persecution of witches, the Spanish Inquisition, the economic and cultural effects of the Inquisition in Europe, and the legacy of the Inquisition.

Arcana Mundi
Magic and the Occult in the Greek and Roman Worlds
Georg Luck

Magic, miracles, demonology, divination, astrology, and alchemy were the *arcana mundi* — the 'secrets of the universe' — of the ancient Greeks and Romans. In this much needed book Georg Luck has provided the general reader and the student with the first comprehensive sourcebook of magic as it was practised by the sorcerers and magi of Greece and Rome.

Professor Luck has gathered together more than 120 key documents from the eight century BC to the fourth century AD. From Homer's *Odyssey* to the 'Great Magical Papyrus of Paris', from Cicero's *On Divination* to a North African curse tablet designed to affect the outcome of a chariot race, the documents are presented in new translations accompanied by a lucid and detailed commentary.

Arcana Mundi uncovers the shadow side of classical civilization and presents a fascinating and at times startling alternative vision of the ancient world.

Georg Luck is Professor of Classics at the Johns Hopkins University. He has served as editor of the *American Journal of Philology* and is the author of *The Latin Love Elegy* and a number of other books and articles dealing with ancient poets and philosophers.

The Templars
Knights of God
Edward Burman

For nearly 200 years, until their suppression in 1312 on charges of heresy and magical practices, the Order of the Poor Knights of the Temple of Solomon — better known as the Templars — were the most formidable and feared fighting machine in Christendom. But besides their military prowess they also possessed immense wealth and political power, becoming bankers and credit brokers to medieval Europe and the allies of kings and popes.

Drawing on contemporary chronicles and original texts, as well as the immense secondary literature, Edward Burman paints a vivid picture of this extraordinary organization of warrior monks and its passage into myth and legend.

Edward Burman read Philosophy at the University of Leeds. He lives and works in Italy and has written a study, in Italian, of the fifteenth-century sculptor Silvestro Aquilano, as well as books on the history of the Inquisition and the Assassins.

Jesus: Essential Readings
New Testament and Apocryphal Teachings Attributed to Jesus
Anthony Duncan

A highly original and challenging anthology of teachings attributed to Jesus, selected from New Testament sources and from apocryphal writings roughly contemporary with the canonical gospels, that present the key themes of Jesus' ministry in a fresh and 'unbiblical' way.

Canon Duncan presents the teachings in the form in which they were probably first communicated: in poetry and symbolic story. Preceded by a helpful introduction outlining the development of the four Gospels and the sources from which they were compiled, the teachings themselves are grouped under thematic headings, each with an introductory essay. The anthology ends with the 'Hymn of Jesus', supposedly sung at the Last Supper.

The Revd Canon Anthony Duncan is Vicar of Warkworth, Northumberland, and an Honorary Canon of Newcastle Cathedral. He is the author of several books on faith and spirituality.

Judaism: The Way of Holiness
The History, Beliefs, Literature, and Observances of the Jewish Faith
Solomon Nigosian

Written for both Jewish and non-Jewish readers, and combining sensitivity to the Jewish heritage with balanced scholarship, this new study crystallizes the unique spirit of Judaism into an engrossing and eloquent account of one of the world's major religions.

Professor Nigosian's account is organized around five main themes that relate to the central Jewish concept of holiness and that unite Jews all over the world in a common understand: Holy God, Holy People, Holy Land, Holy Book and Holy Observances.

'Achieves a high degree of scholarship combined with clarity and readability . . . an absorbing description of this enduringly fascinating people and their beliefs.' — British Book News

Solomon Nigosian is Professor of Religious Studies at the University of Toronto, Canada, and the author of several articles and books on world religions.

A Handbook of Christian Mysticism
An Introduction to the Christian Mystical Tradition
Michael Cox

This wide-ranging introductory survey begins by examining the nature of Christian mysticism, its terminology and antecedents, and goes on to describe its historical development from the New Testament to the twentieth century. It provides concise, accessible summaries of key figures such as St Augustine, Gregory of Nyssa, Dionysius the Areopagite, St Francis, Meister Eckhart, St Bernard and the English mystics of the fourteenth century — Rolle, Hilton, Julian of Norwich and the author of *The Cloud of Unknowing*.

From the flowering of Carmelite mysticism in sixteenth-century Spain, with its two supreme representatives, St Teresa of Avila and St John of the Cross, the third part of the book moves on to offer perspectives on St Francois de Sales and the French School; Protestant mysticism — including Boehme, From the flowering of Carmelite mysticism in sixteenth-century Spain, with

From the flowering of Carmelite mysticism in sixteenth-century Spain, with its two supreme representatives, St Teresa of Avila and St John of the Cross, the third part of the book moves on to offer perspectives on St Francois de Sales and the French School; Protestant mysticism — including Boehme, Law and John Woolman; the mystical element in a number of English poets, from John Donne and George Herbert to Blake and Wordsworth; and two responses to mystical revelation in the modern world — Teilhard de Chardin and Thomas Merton.

The text is supported by a chronological list of mystics and mystical theologians and by an extensive bibliography to aid further study.

'A useful book for those wanting to find their way among names and schools.'—Times Literary Supplement

'A mine of information.' — The Tablet

'Michael Cox's excellent study . . . stresses the uniqueness of Christian mysticism, and with a masterly selection of texts he introduces the reader to virtually every significant Christian mystic from patristic times.' — The Christian Parapsychologist

'If you want information (I do), this is your book . . . I learnt a lot, and shall go on reading and consulting it.' — The Friend

Michael Cox read English at St Catharine's College, Cambridge, and now works in publishing. As well as Christian mysticism his interests include supernatural fiction and he is the biographer of M.R. James, the scholar and ghost story writer.

Dashwood: The Man and the Myth
The Life and Times of the Hell Fire Club's Founder
Eric Towers

In the last twenty years of his life Sir Francis Dashwood (1708–81) became the subject of lurid gossip, and has remained so ever since. Out of convivial meetings with a select group of friends at Medmenham Abbey in Buckinghamshire grew the myth of the Hell Fire Club, whose supposed activities ranged from black magic and devil worship to the ravishing of specially procured virgins. Unsurprisingly, the Medmenham fraternity has fuelled a considerable literature; but is there any factual basis for the Dashwood legend?

This is what Eric Towers sets out to find in this new biography. Far from being the lecher and satanist of popular legend, the real Dashwood emerges as a man of parts — educated, sociable, well-travelled, responsible, and respected by contemporaries as different in outlook as William Pitt and Benjamin Franklin. An active Member of Parliament for twenty years, he became Chancellor of the Exchequer in 1763 and after his elevation to the House of Lords as Lord Le Despenser held the office of Postmaster-General for fifteen years until his death.

Against the colourful background of eighteenth-century politics and society Eric Towers draws on a wide range of primary and secondary material to reconstruct the course of Dashwood's life and travels, his private and public achievements, and the incidents on which the tales of black magic and sex at Medmenham were based. He also shows by whom these tales were spun — and why.

Eric Towers, educated at Newton's Grammar School and Jesus College, Cambridge, combines a career in corporate and public relations with a long interest in eighteenth-century history and culture. He is married and lives in Middlesex.

The Books of the Beast

Essays on Aleister Crowley, Montague Summers, Francis Barrett
and Others

Timothy d'Arch Smith

What connection has Dylan Thomas with a ticket-tout and Kingsley Amis
with a procrastinating pornographer?

What was Montague Summers's dark secret?

Why is *Snowdrops from a Curate's Garden* not quite what it seems?

Who accepted the attentions of both W.B. Yeats *and* George Bernard
Shaw?

Bibliographer and bookseller Timothy d'Arch Smith's long professional
interest in the more curious byways of literature and occultism provides the
answers to these and many other intriguing questions in a collection of witty
and perceptive pen portraits that will delight and inform all connoisseurs of
the unusual.

Here is a gallery of colourful and memorable characters: Aleister
Crowley and his 'magickal' first editions; Montague Summers, with his
simultaneous obsession with and loathing of the black arts; R.A. Caton,
Summers's reclusive and eccentric publisher; Ralph Chubb, homosexual
visionary; Francis Barrett, author of *The Magus*; Florence Farr, actress and
occultist; and the world of pornography as reflected in the British Library's
celebrated 'private case' of erotica.

Finally in what he modestly calls an 'eminently skippable' Epilogue,
Timothy d'Arch Smith reveals something of himself and those — from
Crowley's disciple 'Fra N. ·.'to a peer with specialized reading requirements
— with whom his career and interests have brought him into contact.

Dracula's Brood
Rare Vampire Stories by Friends and Contemporaries of Bram Stoker
Selected and Introduced by Richard Dalby

The most famous vampire tale of them all is Bram Stoker's *Dracula*, published in 1897. But it was not the first piece of fiction to describe the doings of the undead, and it was by no means the last.

This unique anthology gathers together twenty-six rare vampire stories written by friends and contemporaries of Bram Stoker between 1865 and 1940 — including a gory *tour de force* by Stoker himself, 'The Dualitists', reprinted here for the first time since its publication in 1886.

Richard Dalby has deliberately avoided stories that have been regularly reprinted and has concentrated instead on reviving neglected examples of the vampire genre — ranging from Frederick Cowles' beautiful but deadly Princess Bessenyei to tales of vampiric trees and even of a sinister tortoise bent on vengeance. A similarly wide range of authors is represented, including Sir Arthur Conan Doyle, Algernon Blackwood, Julian Hawthorne (son of Nathaniel), Vernon Lee, William Gilbert (father of W.S. Gilbert), Eliza Lynn Linton, and W.F. Harvey.

Dracula's Brood provides a veritable feast of pleasure for all lovers of supernatual and fantasy fiction. It also throws new light on a small but fertile corner of Victorian and early twentieth-century literature.

Richard Dalby is a professional author, bibliographer, researcher, and book dealer specializing in supernatural fiction. His previous books include *The Best Ghost Stories of H. Russell Wakefield*.

The Occult Roots of Nazism
The Ariosophists of Austria and Germany 1890–1935
Nicholas Goodrick-Clarke

Nearly half a century after the defeat of the Third Reich the complexities and ramifications of Nazi ideology are still being unravelled.

One key element in any attempt to understand Nazism and the power it wielded is its association with the occult and millenarian sub-culture of late imperial Germany and Austria. Until now this has been the subject of superficially researched and often sensationalized works: this book — for the first time — offers historians and general readers alike an accurate, meticulously documented account of the proto-Nazi context in relation to occult and racist fantasies.

Nicholas Goodrick-Clarke takes as his main focus the lives, doctrines, and cult activities of the Ariosophists — in particular Guido von List (1848-1919) and Jörg Lanz von Liebenfels (1874-1954). The Ariosophists combined *völkisch* nationalism and 'Aryan' racism with occultism to support their advocacy of German world-rule. Although they were only marginally active in practical politics their ideas and symbols filtered through to nationalist-racist groups associated with the infant Nazi party, and in time exerted a strong influence on Himmler's SS.

Ariosophical doctrines advocated the rule of gnostic/élites and orders, the stratification of society according to racial purity and occult initiation, the ruthless subjugation and ultimate destruction of non-German inferiors, and the foundation of a pan-German world-empire. Such fantasies were actualized with terrifying consequences in the Third Reich: Auschwitz, Sobibor and Treblinka are the hellish museums of Nazi apocalyptic, the roots of which lay in the millennial visions of Ariosophy.

The story of Ariosophy is a bizarre and compulsively fascinating one. It also contains lessons we cannot afford to ignore. In Nicholas Goodrick-Clarke it has found its definitive historian.

'*Serious appraisal of occultism demands not only rigorous scholarship but penetrating critical faculties to explore the delicate distinction between fact and fantasy. Nicholas Goodrick-Clarke has just these qualities — and more.*' — Dr Bryan Wilson, All Souls College, Oxford

'*At last, a study of the occult underworlds connected with the prehistory of German National Socialism and, furthermore, based upon painstaking research rather than speculative inventions.*' — Ellic Howe, author of *Astrology and the Third Reich*

'*All students of twentieth-century ideology will welcome this scholarly and dis-passionate treatment of a subject that is all too often sensationalized.*' — Dr Peter Pulzer, Gladstone Professor of Government, University of Oxford